ideals

HERSHEY'S® Chocolate and Cocoa COOKBOOK

Bonanza Books
New York, N.Y.

Introduction

Hershey Foods Corporation is world famous for its contribution to the wonderful world of chocolate. A tremendous variety of eating and baking products have made Hershey a household name for generations. Within these pages you will find an outstanding selection of recipes using Hershey's many superb baking products.

We've selected a mouth-watering assortment of recipes for your eating pleasure, ranging from traditional favorites (Hershey's Cocoa Fudge) to variations of a basic recipe (Deluxe Marbled Brownies) to marvelous company treats (Chocolate Banana Cream Pie)! The Microwave chapter offers many taste-tempting, time-saving suggestions sure to please family and friends.

We hope that you enjoy these delicious ideas for fabulous snacks, desserts, candies, breads, and beverages!

Contents

ISBN: 0-517-379252

The Hershey Logo is a Trademark of Hershey Foods Corporation, Ideals Publishing Corporation, Licensee.

Copyright © MCMLXXXII by Hershey Foods Corporation. All rights reserved. Printed and bound in the United States of America.

Cover Recipes: Hershey's Sweet Chocolate Cake, p. 33 with Seven-Minute Frosting, p. 37
Peanut Blossoms, p. 8
Deluxe Marbled Brownies, p. 16
Velvety Chocolate Cream Pie, p. 22

THIS EDITION IS PUBLISHED BY BONANZA BOOKS, A DIVISION OF CROWN PUBLISHERS, INC. BY ARRANGEMENT WITH IDEALS PUBLISHING CORPORATION. BONANZA 1982 EDITION MANUFACTURED IN THE UNITED STATES OF AMERICA.

Associate Editor and Food Stylist Susan Noland

Chocolate and Cocoa Basics

Storage of Chocolate Products

Since chocolate contains cocoa butter, temperatures of 78°F and above cause chocolate to melt and cocoa butter to rise to the surface, forming a gray discoloration known as "cocoa butter bloom." "Sugar bloom" may occur when condensation forms on the surface of semi-sweet or milk chocolate, causing sugar to dissolve and rise to the surface. In both cases, the quality and flavor of the chocolate is not affected. Upon melting, the chocolate regains its original color. Chocolate products generally stay fresh well over a year when stored correctly. To avoid bloom, store chocolate in a cool, dry place where the temperature is about 70°F. Chocolate can be refrigerated during hot, humid weather, but in some instances it may "bloom" when brought to room temperature.

Hershey's Baking Chocolate should be stored at room temperature but can be refrigerated during hot weather because it contains no sugar and will not develop sugar bloom. Hershey's Cocoa, Instant and Hot Cocoa Mix keep very well when stored at room temperature in tightly sealed containers. Store opened cans of Hershey's Chocolate Flavored Syrup and Hershey's Fudge Topping in refrigerator.

Melting Hints

1. Break or cut chocolate into 1-inch pieces prior to placing in top of a double boiler.
2. Melt milk chocolate in top of double boiler over warm water.
3. Melt semi-sweet chocolate in top of a double boiler over hot, not boiling, water.
4. Melt unsweetened baking chocolate in top of a double boiler over simmering water.
5. Melt peanut butter chips in the top of a double boiler over hot, not boiling, water. If melted chips become grainy or too thick, add 1 tablespoon shortening or vegetable oil to each 6 ounces of chips; stir to blend. Return to heat (over hot water) if necessary.
6. Thoroughly wash and dry double boiler after each use. Residue will affect taste of chocolate.
7. Regulate heat carefully! Chocolate scorches easily!

Garnish with Chocolate

Alleghetti Frosting (sometimes called Shadow Icing) is an easy way to dress up plain frosting. In a small saucepan combine 1 square (1 ounce) unsweetened chocolate and ½ teaspoon shortening. Heat over low heat, stirring constantly. Drizzle melted chocolate from a teaspoon around the edge of the cake to form "icicles."

Curls: Draw blade of vegetable parer over smooth side of a slightly warm block of unsweetened baking chocolate or a dark, sweet chocolate bar.

Cutouts: Melt 4 ounces semi-sweet and 1 ounce unsweetened chocolate in the top of a double boiler over boiling water. Remove from heat, let cool 5 minutes, and stir with a wooden spoon until pan is cool to your touch.

Line cookie sheet with waxed paper and spread chocolate ³⁄₁₆ inch thick. Let cool until almost set. Press designs into chocolate, using cookie cutters. Peel paper from back of shape. Store on waxed paper in refrigerator.

Leaves: Gather 20 to 25 medium-size leaves with stems (English ivy, elm, dogwood). Wash and dry thoroughly. Melt 1 cup semi-sweet chocolate chips in top of double boiler over hot, not boiling, water. Remove from heat; keep over warm water. Carefully brush a thin layer (about ⅛ inch thick) of chocolate on underside of leaf. Chocolate and leaf will separate more easily if edges are not covered. Place coated leaves on wire rack until firm; chill if necessary. Carefully peel leaf from coating; store in cool place or refrigerator.

Tempering Hershey Products for Coating Candies

Have you ever wondered why commercially made chocolate-coated candy stays so glossy and firm at room temperature? It is because of a process called tempering. Tempering is achieved by heating and cooling chocolate to specific temperatures, causing cocoa butter crystal formation so that the chocolate coating will stay firm and glossy without the addition of wax or refrigeration of the coated candy. Although Hershey Chocolate is tempered during manufacturing, melting it destroys this temper; thus this process must be repeated by the consumer.

Carefully read all tips and instructions before beginning. Set aside about 2 to 3 hours to complete the process. The most important thing to remember is that the process (temperature changes) must happen evenly and slowly, with constant stirring. *It cannot be rushed.* Do not try to temper chocolate and coat candy on a humid day. Humidity, steam, wet pans, or utensils cause chocolate to thicken, tighten and become grainy. Even a few drops of water can cause problems, so make sure all utensils are dry before beginning.

Candies coated with chocolate that is *not* tempered will probably have a somewhat sticky coating that will "bloom." Bloom is white or gray spots or streaks caused by separation of the sugar or fat particles from the chocolate. Chocolate that has bloom is not harmful and does not taste different, but may look unappetizing.

Chocolate and Cocoa Basics

Tempering Instructions

1. Melt proper amount of chocolate and vegetable shortening in a small bowl set in a pan of very warm water. Make sure water level is 2 to 3 inches below rim of bowl. (Water temperature should not be above 120°F).
2. Heat chocolate to 108°F, stirring constantly with rubber spatula; scrape down sides and bottom of bowl frequently so that the chocolate is evenly and uniformly heated.
3. When chocolate reaches 108°F, remove bowl from pan of water. Stir frequently until chocolate cools to 85°F. Continue stirring and scraping bowl constantly until chocolate cools to 80°F.
4. Keep chocolate at 80°F, stirring constantly, for 10 minutes. This is important because it develops the crystals necessary for gloss. It may be necessary to briefly set bowl in warm water to maintain temperature.
5. Rewarm chocolate in pan of warm water to 86°F; hold at that temperature for 5 minutes before dipping.
6. *Important:* Keep chocolate at 86°F during entire dipping process. If temperature at this point goes below 84°, the entire tempering process must be repeated from Step #2.
7. Centers must be removed from refrigerator and allowed to reach room temperature before coating. (Dipping chilled centers may result in cracked coating and/or bloom on the coating.)
8. Dip room temperature centers or confections completely in tempered, melted chocolate. Dip one at a time using fork, fondue fork, or hat pin. Gently tap fork on side of bowl to remove excess chocolate. Invert onto waxed paper-covered tray; swirl small amount of coating over utensil marks.
9. Chill coated candies a maximum of 15 minutes in refrigerator to help coating harden. Remove promptly or bloom may occur.
10. Store coated candies at room temperature (60°-75°F), but keep them well covered.

Important Tips for Making Candy

1. The process is not difficult, but it does take time. Remember that "practice makes perfect." It becomes easier each time you do it.
2. It is critical that you do not try to rush the process or skip steps. Key words are slowly, evenly, and uniformly.
3. Use a candy thermometer which registers from 70°F to 110°F. Most will not work since they do not register below 100°F; laboratory thermometers do register temperatures in the appropriate range. The thermometer is critical to the process; you will not get good results without it.
   Test thermometer for accuracy by placing it in a pan of boiling water. An accurate thermometer will register 212°F at sea level. Add or subtract degrees from cooking temperatures in recipes according to the thermometer reading.
   To get an accurate reading, be sure that your candy thermometer is standing upright and that the bulb is covered by liquid. The bulb should not be resting on the bottom of the pan.
4. The chocolate mixture should be fluid at 108°F. If chocolate becomes tight or grainy due to humidity, stir in a small amount of solid vegetable shortening, one teaspoonful at a time, until chocolate is smooth and fluid again. At this point, retemper chocolate.
5. Use Step #4 only as an emergency measure. Do not purposely try to extend chocolate coatings with extra fat and/or water. This will ruin your coating.
6. Constant scraping and stirring as stated in the instructions will help insure success and is necessary for proper crystal formation.
7. Use solid vegetable shortening as directed, *not* butter or margarine. Butter and margarine contain moisture that will cause chocolate to tighten and become grainy.

Temperatures and Tests for Syrup and Candies

Test of Doneness	Final Temperature of Syrup at Sea Level*	Description of Test
Thread	230 to 234°F	Syrup spins a 2-inch thread when dropped from fork or spoon.
Soft ball	234 to 240°F	Syrup, when dropped into very cold water, forms a soft ball which flattens on removal from water.
Firm ball	244 to 248°F	Syrup, when dropped into very cold water, forms a firm ball which does not flatten on removal from water.
Hard ball	250 to 266°F	Syrup, when dropped into very cold water, forms a ball which is hard enough to hold its shape, yet plastic.
Soft crack	270 to 290°F	Syrup, when dropped into very cold water, separates into threads which are hard but not brittle.
Hard crack	300 to 310°F	Syrup, when dropped into very cold water, separates into threads which are hard and brittle.

*For each 500 feet of elevation, cook the syrup to a temperature 1° lower than temperature called for at sea level.

Handbook for Food Preparation   Eighth Edition © 1980
American Home Economics Association

Chocolate and Cocoa Basics

Glossary of Chocolate and Cocoa Products

Artificial or Synthetic Chocolate: An imitation product which contains no cocoa bean derived ingredients. In the extreme, it can mean no milk or sugar either—all replacement ingredients. Hershey produces no artificial chocolate.

Bitter Chocolate: (Commonly referred to as unsweetened, baking, or cooking chocolate). Chocolate liquor which has been cooled and molded, usually in blocks.

Cacao (cocoa) Beans: The source of cocoa and chocolate, cacao beans are the fruit of the cacao tree, which grows only 20° north or south of the equator and mainly in West Africa and Latin America.

Cacao Nibs: The "meat" of the cacao bean. After the beans are cleaned and roasted at controlled temperatures to bring out the full flavor and aroma, the outer shells are removed, leaving the nibs.

Chocolate: Although legally this means unsweetened (bitter) chocolate or chocolate liquor (see below), common usage implies milk chocolate, semi-sweet chocolate, and sweet chocolate.

Chocolate Flavored: This term is used for food products flavored with cocoa and/or chocolate liquor, but not containing enough of these substances to be called chocolate as defined by the Standards of Identity (see below).

Chocolate Flavored Syrup: Commonly referred to as chocolate syrup. A combination, in varying proportions, of chocolate liquor or cocoa, sugar, water, salt, and sometimes other flavorings such as vanilla.

Chocolate Liquor: Base material of all chocolate products. The nibs, which contain more than 50% cocoa butter, are ground by a process which generates enough heat to liquify the cocoa butter and form chocolate liquor. Chocolate liquor has no alcoholic content.

Cocoa Butter: A vegetable fat extracted from chocolate liquor by "pressing" at high pressure. The distinctive melting properties of cocoa butter give chocolate products their satisfying texture.

Cocoa Powder: The dry substance of chocolate liquor that remains after most of the cocoa butter has been extracted.

Cocoa Powder (Dutch Process): Cocoa powder from nibs or chocolate liquor which has been treated with alkali to neutralize the natural acids. Dutch Process cocoa is darker, and the flavor slightly different from that of the so-called natural cocoa.

Compound Chocolate: A term used in the chocolate industry for chocolate-like products in which most or all of the cocoa butter has been removed and replaced by another vegetable fat. Frequently referred to as "white chocolate" or confectioners' coating by consumers, it is available in dark, white, or pastel colors.

Milk Chocolate: A combination of chocolate liquor, added cocoa butter, sugar, and milk or cream. It must contain at least 10% chocolate liquor. It may also contain optional ingredients.

Premelted Baking Chocolate-Type Product: A mixture of unsweetened cocoa and vegetable oil in foil or plastic envelopes.

Semi-Sweet Chocolate: A combination of chocolate liquor, added cocoa butter, and sugar. It must contain at least 35% chocolate liquor. Most commonly known in the form of semi-sweet chocolate chips.

Sweet (Dark) Chocolate: A combination of chocolate liquor, added cocoa butter, and sugar. It must contain at least 15% chocolate liquor and has a higher proportion of sugar than semi-sweet chocolate.

Standards of Identity: A rigid set of identifications, as established by the Food and Drug Administration (FDA), which designates for each chocolate and cocoa product the percentage of key ingredients that must be present in order for them to bear the name of such product.

Substitutions

For Baking Chocolate: 3 tablespoons cocoa plus 1 tablespoon shortening or oil equals 1 square (1 ounce) baking chocolate.

For Premelted Unsweetened Chocolate: 3 tablespoons cocoa plus 1 tablespoon oil or melted shortening equals 1 envelope (1 ounce) pre-melted unsweetened chocolate.

For Semi-sweet Chocolate: 6 tablespoons cocoa plus 7 tablespoons sugar plus ¼ cup shortening equals 1 6-ounce package (1 cup) semi-sweet chocolate chips or 6 squares (1 ounce each) semi-sweet chocolate.

For Sweet Cooking Chocolate: 3 tablespoons cocoa plus 4½ tablespoons sugar plus 2⅔ tablespoons shortening equals 1 4-ounce bar sweet cooking chocolate.

Note: In these substitutions, don't use butter or margarine. They contain a slight amount of water, which could cause ingredients to separate.

There are three easy ways to use cocoa in recipes that originally called for another chocolate product:

1. Combine cocoa (and sugar) with the dry ingredients. Add the extra shortening with the shortening called for in the recipe.

2. Melt the extra shortening. Remove from heat and blend in cocoa. If you're using oil, merely blend oil and cocoa. Add mixture to the recipe as you would premelted unsweetened chocolate.

3. For extra cocoa flavor and color, add the extra shortening with the shortening called for in the recipe. Mix cocoa and part of the water called for in the recipe into a smooth paste. Add to the creamed mixture.

Cookies

Basic Cookie Mix

Makes approximately 11 cups.

> 5 cups unsifted all-purpose flour
> 2 cups granulated sugar
> 1 cup packed brown sugar
> 2 tablespoons baking powder
> 1 tablespoon salt
> 1 cup shortening
> ½ cup butter

Combine flour, granulated sugar, brown sugar, baking powder, and salt in a large bowl. (You can use an electric mixer on slow speed for mixing.) Add shortening and butter; cut in with pastry blender or hands until mixture resembles coarse cornmeal. Store in an airtight container in refrigerator.

Note: After refrigeration, measure amount of mix needed; bring to room temperature for easier blending.

Peanutty Chewy Bars

Makes 24.

> 2½ cups Basic Cookie Mix (Recipe above)
> ⅓ cup Hershey's Cocoa
> ⅓ cup granulated sugar
> 2 eggs, lightly beaten
> 1 cup Reese's Peanut Butter Chips
> 1⅓ cups (14-ounce can) sweetened condensed milk
> 1 cup flaked coconut

Combine cookie mix, cocoa, sugar, and eggs in a large bowl; blend well. Spread in a greased 13 x 9 x 2-inch baking pan. Bake at 350° for 8 to 10 minutes or until mixture is set. Remove from oven. Sprinkle peanut butter chips over top. Drizzle sweetened condensed milk evenly over chips; top with coconut. Return to oven; bake for 20 to 25 minutes or until lightly browned on top. Cool in pan. Cut into bars.

Cherry Chocolate Chip Cookies

Makes approximately 2½ dozen.

> 2½ cups Basic Cookie Mix (Recipe above)
> ¼ cup sour cream
> ¼ cup finely chopped, well-drained maraschino cherries
> 1 cup Hershey's Semi-Sweet Chocolate Chips
> 1 cup chopped nuts
> 30 maraschino cherry halves, well drained

Stir together cookie mix, sour cream, cherries, and chocolate chips in a large bowl. Shape into 1-inch balls; roll in nuts. Place on a greased cookie sheet. Garnish each with a cherry half. Bake at 375° for 8 to 10 minutes. Remove from cookie sheet; cool on a wire rack.

Sugar Cookies

Makes approximately 2 dozen.

> 3 cups Basic Cookie Mix (Recipe on this page)
> 1 egg plus 1 egg yolk, lightly beaten
> 1 teaspoon vanilla
> 1 egg white, lightly beaten

Combine cookie mix, egg, egg yolk, and vanilla in a small bowl. Cover; chill until firm, about 3 hours. Divide dough in half; roll each half to desired thickness on a lightly floured surface. Cut into desired shapes; brush with egg white. Place on a greased cookie sheet. Bake at 375° for 8 to 10 minutes or until lightly browned. (Cookies spread considerably during baking.) Remove from cookie sheet. Cool on a wire rack.

Variations

Surprise Cookies Makes approximately 1½ dozen: Roll dough on a lightly floured surface to ¼ inch thick. Cut into 2½-inch circles. Place on a greased cookie sheet. Break a ½ pound Hershey's Milk Chocolate Bar into squares. Place a square in the center of each circle; place another circle on top. Seal edges with the tines of a fork. (Reserve remaining chocolate squares for Pinwheels below.) Bake at 375° for 10 to 12 minutes. Remove from cookie sheet. Cool on a wire rack.

Pinwheels Makes approximately 3 dozen: Melt 4 ounces of a Hershey's Milk Chocolate Bar or remaining squares from the Surprise Cookies above; cool. Divide dough in half; roll out each half into a rectangle on a lightly floured surface to ¼-inch thickness. Spread with melted chocolate; roll up dough from the long side. Wrap dough in plastic; refrigerate until well chilled. Cut into ¼-inch slices. Place on a greased cookie sheet. Bake at 375° for 8 to 10 minutes. Remove from cookie sheet. Cool on a wire rack.

Basic Cookie Mix Variations: Cherry Chocolate Chip Cookies, above
Pinwheels, above
Peanutty Chewy Bars, above

Cookies

Peanut Blossoms

Makes approximately 4 dozen.

- ½ cup shortening
- ¾ cup peanut butter
- ⅓ cup granulated sugar
- ⅓ cup packed brown sugar
- 1 egg
- 2 tablespoons milk
- 1 teaspoon vanilla
- 1½ cups unsifted all-purpose flour
- 1 teaspoon baking soda
- ½ teaspoon salt
- Granulated sugar
- 1 9-ounce package (about 54) Hershey's Milk Chocolate Kisses

Cream shortening and peanut butter in large bowl. Blend in granulated sugar and brown sugar. Add egg, milk, and vanilla; beat well. In a separate bowl combine flour, baking soda, and salt. Gradually add flour mixture to creamed mixture; blend thoroughly. Shape dough into 1-inch balls. Roll in granulated sugar. Place on an ungreased cookie sheet. Bake at 375° for 10 to 12 minutes. Remove from oven. Immediately place an *unwrapped* Kiss on top of each cookie, pressing down so that cookie cracks around the edges. Remove from cookie sheet. Cool on a wire rack.

Crunchy Oatmeal Peanut Butter Chip Cookies

Makes approximately 5 dozen.

- ¾ cup butter *or* margarine
- 1 cup packed brown sugar
- ½ cup granulated sugar
- 1 egg
- 1 teaspoon vanilla
- 1 cup unsifted all-purpose flour
- ½ teaspoon baking soda
- ½ teaspoon salt
- ¼ cup milk
- 2½ cups quick-cooking rolled oats
- 2 cups (12-ounce package) Reese's Peanut Butter Chips

Cream butter *or* margarine, brown sugar, granulated sugar, egg, and vanilla in large bowl. In a separate bowl combine flour, baking soda, and salt. Alternately beat in flour mixture and milk to creamed mixture. Stir in oats and peanut butter chips. Drop by teaspoonfuls onto a greased cookie sheet. Bake at 375° for 10 to 12 minutes or until light brown. Remove from cookie sheet. Cool on a wire rack.

Double Peanut Butter Cookies

Makes approximately 3½ dozen.

- ¼ cup butter *or* margarine
- ¼ cup shortening
- ½ cup peanut butter
- ½ cup granulated sugar
- ½ cup packed brown sugar
- 1 egg
- 1¼ cups unsifted all-purpose flour
- ¾ teaspoon baking soda
- ½ teaspoon baking powder
- ¼ teaspoon salt
- 2 cups (12-ounce package) Reese's Peanut Butter Chips

Cream butter *or* margarine, shortening, peanut butter, sugar, brown sugar, and egg in a large bowl. Blend in flour, baking soda, baking powder, and salt. Stir in peanut butter chips. Shape into 1-inch balls. Place on an ungreased cookie sheet. Flatten in a criss-cross pattern with a fork dipped in sugar. Bake at 375° for 10 to 12 minutes or until set. Cool several minutes before removing from cookie sheet onto a wire rack.

Macaroon Kiss Cookies

Makes approximately 4½ dozen.

- ⅓ cup butter *or* margarine
- 1 3-ounce package cream cheese
- ¾ cup granulated sugar
- 1 egg yolk
- 2 teaspoons almond extract
- 2 teaspoons brandy
- 1¼ cups unsifted all-purpose flour
- 2 teaspoons baking powder
- ¼ teaspoon salt
- 5 cups (14-ounce package) flaked coconut
- 1 9-ounce package (about 54) Hershey's Milk Chocolate Kisses

Cream butter *or* margarine, cream cheese, and sugar in a large bowl. Add egg yolk, almond extract, and brandy; beat well. In a separate bowl, combine flour, baking powder, and salt. Gradually add flour mixture to creamed mixture; blend well. Stir in 3 cups of the flaked coconut. Chill dough about 1 hour. Shape dough into 1-inch balls. Roll balls in the remaining 2 cups coconut. Place on an ungreased cookie sheet; flatten with a fork. Bake at 350° for 12 to 15 minutes or until lightly browned on the bottoms. Remove from oven. Press an *unwrapped* Kiss into the center of each cookie; return to oven for 15 seconds. Carefully remove cookies from cookie sheet.

Chocolate Drop Cookies

Makes approximately 4 dozen.

- ⅔ cup butter or margarine, softened
- 1 cup granulated sugar
- 1½ teaspoons vanilla
- 1 egg
- 1½ cups unsifted all-purpose flour
- ½ cup Hershey's Cocoa
- ½ teaspoon baking soda
- ¼ teaspoon salt
- ⅓ cup buttermilk or sour milk*

Cream butter or margarine and granulated sugar in large bowl. Blend in vanilla and egg. In a separate bowl combine flour, cocoa, baking soda, and salt. Alternately add flour mixture and buttermilk or sour milk to creamed mixture. Drop by teaspoonfuls 2 inches apart onto a lightly greased cookie sheet. Bake at 350° for 7 to 9 minutes. Remove from cookie sheet. Cool on a wire rack. Frost, if desired.

*To Sour Milk: Use 1 teaspoon vinegar plus milk to equal ⅓ cup.

Chocolate Rum Balls

Makes approximately 4 dozen.

- 3¼ cups (12-ounce package) crushed vanilla wafers
- ¾ cup confectioners' sugar
- ¼ cup Hershey's Cocoa
- 1½ cups chopped nuts
- 3 tablespoons light corn syrup
- ½ cup rum or ½ cup orange juice plus 1 teaspoon grated orange peel
  Confectioners' sugar

Combine vanilla wafer crumbs, confectioners' sugar, cocoa, and nuts in a large bowl. Blend in corn syrup, rum or orange juice, and grated peel. Shape into 1-inch balls. Roll in confectioners' sugar. Store in an airtight container several days to develop flavor. Roll again in confectioners' sugar before serving.

Thumbprint Kiss Cookies

Makes approximately 2 dozen.

- 1 egg, lightly beaten
- 1 teaspoon vanilla
- 2½ cups Chocolate Cookie Mix (Recipe on page 12)
  Chopped nuts
- 24 Hershey's Milk Chocolate Kisses
  Vanilla Frosting (Recipe on page 12)

Combine first three ingredients in a bowl; blend well. Form into 1-inch balls. Roll each in chopped nuts. Place on a cookie sheet. Press down center of each with your thumb. Bake at 375° for 8 to 10 minutes. Remove from oven. Place a dot of Vanilla Frosting in center of each cookie. Immediately press an *unwrapped* Kiss into frosting. Remove from cookie sheet; cool on a wire rack.

Holiday Chocolate Drop Cookies

Makes approximately 3 dozen.

- ½ cup butter or margarine
- 1¼ cups packed brown sugar
- 2 eggs
- ¼ cup Hershey's Cocoa
- 1½ cups unsifted all-purpose flour
- ½ teaspoon baking soda
- ¼ teaspoon salt
- 1 teaspoon vanilla
- ½ cup snipped dates
- 1 cup raisins
- ½ cup chopped walnuts

Cream butter or margarine and sugar in a large bowl. Add eggs; beat well. In a separate bowl combine cocoa, flour, baking soda, and salt. Blend flour mixture into creamed mixture. Add vanilla, dates, raisins, and walnuts. Chill for 30 minutes. Drop by teaspoonfuls onto a lightly greased cookie sheet. Bake at 350° for 8 to 10 minutes or until set. Remove from cookie sheet. Cool on a wire rack.

Peanut Butter Chip Cookies

Makes approximately 5 dozen.

- 1 cup shortening or ¾ cup butter or margarine
- 1 cup granulated sugar
- ½ cup packed light brown sugar
- 1 teaspoon vanilla
- 2 eggs
- 2 cups unsifted all-purpose flour
- 1 teaspoon baking soda
- 2 cups (12-ounce package) Reese's Peanut Butter Chips

Cream shortening or butter or margarine, granulated sugar, brown sugar, and vanilla in a large bowl. Add eggs; beat well. In a separate bowl combine flour and baking soda. Gradually add flour to creamed mixture; blend well. Stir in peanut butter chips. Drop by teaspoonfuls onto an ungreased cookie sheet. Bake at 350° for 10 to 12 minutes or until light brown. Cool slightly on cookie sheet before removing to a wire rack.

Hoot Owl Cookies

Makes approximately 2½ dozen.

- ¾ cup butter *or* margarine
- 1 cup packed brown sugar
- 1 egg
- 1½ teaspoons vanilla
- 2¼ cups unsifted all-purpose flour
- 2 teaspoons baking powder
- ½ teaspoon salt
- ⅓ cup Hershey's Cocoa
- ¼ teaspoon baking soda
- 1 tablespoon water
- ¼ cup Reese's Peanut Butter Chips
- ½ cup whole cashew nuts

Cream butter *or* margarine, brown sugar, egg, and vanilla in large bowl. In a separate bowl, combine flour, baking powder, and salt. Blend flour mixture into creamed mixture. Remove two-thirds of the dough to a floured surface. In small bowl combine cocoa and baking soda; add to remaining dough. Blend water into chocolate dough.

Roll half of the vanilla dough into a 10 x 4-inch rectangle. Shape half of chocolate dough into a roll 10 inches long; place in center of rectangle of vanilla dough. Mold sides of vanilla dough around roll of chocolate dough. Repeat shaping steps with remaining dough. Wrap in plastic wrap; chill at least 2 hours or overnight.

Cut dough into ⅛-inch thick slices; lay two slices together side-by-side on a greased cookie sheet. Pinch a corner of each slice to form ears. Place a peanut butter chip in the center of each slice for eyes; press a cashew nut between slices for a beak. Bake at 350° for 8 to 10 minutes or until set. Remove from cookie sheet; cool on rack.

Peanut Butter & Jelly Thumbprints

Makes approximately 5 dozen.

- 1 cup butter *or* margarine
- 1¾ cups packed brown sugar
- 2 eggs
- 2 teaspoons vanilla
- 3 cups unsifted all-purpose flour
- 1 teaspoon baking powder
- 1 teaspoon salt
- 2 cups (12-ounce package) Reese's Peanut Butter Chips
- 1½ cups quick-cooking rolled oats
- ¾ cup jelly *or* preserves (apple, grape, peach, etc.)

Cream butter *or* margarine and brown sugar in large bowl. Add eggs and vanilla; beat until light and fluffy. In a separate bowl combine flour, baking powder, and salt. Gradually add flour mixture to creamed mixture. Reserve ½ cup peanut butter chips. Stir in oats and 1½ cups peanut butter chips. Shape dough into 1-inch balls. Place balls on an ungreased cookie sheet. Press the center of each with your thumb to make a deep depression about 1 inch wide. Bake at 400° for 7 to 9 minutes or until lightly browned. Remove from cookie sheet. Cool on a wire rack. Fill center of each cookie with ½ teaspoon jelly *or* preserves; top with several of the reserved peanut butter chips.

No-Bake Peanut Butter Chip Cookies

Makes approximately 4 dozen.

- 2 cups (12-ounce package) Reese's Peanut Butter Chips
- 1 tablespoon shortening
- 5 cups cornflakes cereal, coarsely crushed
- 1 cup raisins

Melt peanut butter chips and shortening in top of a double boiler over hot, *not* boiling, water. Stir until smooth and creamy. Combine cereal, melted chips, and raisins; stir until cereal is coated. Drop by teaspoonfuls onto a waxed paper-lined cookie sheet. Cover and chill for 1 hour.

Hershey's Chocolate Chip Cookies

Makes approximately 6 dozen.

- 1 cup butter *or* margarine, softened
- ¾ cup packed brown sugar
- ¾ cup granulated sugar
- 2 eggs
- 1 teaspoon vanilla
- 2¼ cups unsifted all-purpose flour
- 1 teaspoon baking soda
- ½ teaspoon salt
- 1 cup chopped nuts
- 2 cups (12-ounce package) Hershey's Semi-Sweet Chocolate Chips

Cream butter *or* margarine, brown sugar, granulated sugar, eggs, and vanilla in a large bowl. In a separate bowl combine flour, baking soda, and salt. Blend into creamed mixture. Stir in nuts and chocolate chips. Drop by teaspoonfuls onto an ungreased cookie sheet. Bake at 375° for 8 to 10 minutes or until light brown. Cool slightly on cookie sheet before removing to a wire rack.

Cookies

Maple-Nut Chocolate Brownies

Makes 16.

- 2 eggs
- 1 cup granulated sugar
- ½ teaspoon vanilla
- ½ cup butter *or* margarine, melted
- ½ cup unsifted all-purpose flour
- ¼ teaspoon baking powder
- ¼ teaspoon salt
- ⅓ cup chopped nuts
- ¾ teaspoon maple flavoring
- ¼ cup Hershey's Cocoa
- Confectioners' sugar, optional

Beat eggs in small bowl. Gradually add sugar and vanilla. Blend in melted butter *or* margarine; beat well. In a separate bowl combine flour, baking powder, and salt. Gradually add to creamed mixture; blend thoroughly. Remove 1 cup of the batter; stir in chopped nuts and maple flavoring. Add cocoa to remaining batter; blend thoroughly. Spoon into a greased 8-inch square baking pan in 4 alternate rows, i.e. chocolate-maple-chocolate-maple. Use a rubber spatula or scraper to zigzag lightly through the batter, being careful not to blend too well. Bake at 350° for 35 to 40 minutes or until brownie begins to pull away from edges of pan. Cool in pan. Sprinkle lightly with confectioners' sugar, if desired. Cut into squares.

Chocolate Cookie Mix

Makes approximately 11 cups.

- 4 cups unsifted all-purpose flour
- 4 cups granulated sugar
- 1⅓ cups Hershey's Cocoa
- 2 teaspoons baking powder
- 1 teaspoon salt
- 1½ cups butter *or* margarine

Combine thoroughly flour, sugar, cocoa, baking powder, and salt in a large bowl. (An electric mixer on slow speed can be used for mixing.) Add butter *or* margarine; cut in with a pastry blender or with hands until mixture resembles coarse cornmeal. Store in an airtight container in refrigerator.

Note: After refrigeration, measure amount of mix needed; bring to room temperature for easier blending.

Chewy Chocolate Wafers

Makes approximately 3 dozen.

- 1 egg, lightly beaten
- 1 teaspoon vanilla
- 2½ cups Chocolate Cookie Mix (Recipe on this page)

Combine all ingredients in a bowl; blend well. Place on waxed paper. Shape into a log about 8 inches long. Wrap tightly in waxed paper. Refrigerate for 30 minutes. Reshape log to keep it round. Chill until firm. Slice ⅛ inch thick. Place on a lightly greased cookie sheet. Bake at 375° for 5 to 7 minutes or until set. Remove from cookie sheet. Cool on a wire rack. Frost with Vanilla Frosting, if desired.

Vanilla Frosting

- 1 cup confectioners' sugar
- 1 tablespoon shortening
- 1 to 2 tablespoons milk
- ½ teaspoon vanilla

Combine all ingredients in a small bowl. Beat until spreading consistency.

Brownies

Makes 16.

- 2 eggs
- 1 teaspoon vanilla
- 3 cups Chocolate Cookie Mix (Recipe on this page)
- ½ cup chopped nuts

Combine eggs and vanilla in a large bowl; beat lightly. Add cookie mix and chopped nuts. Stir until ingredients are well blended. Spoon into a greased, 8-inch square baking pan. Bake at 350° for 25 to 30 minutes or until brownie begins to pull away from sides of pan. (Do not overbake.) Cool in pan. Frost with Mint Frosting, if desired. Cut into bars.

Mint Frosting

- 1½ cups confectioners' sugar
- 2 tablespoons milk
- 1 tablespoon shortening
- ½ teaspoon vanilla
- ⅛ teaspoon pure mint *or* peppermint extract
- 2 or 3 drops green food color, optional

Combine all ingredients in the order listed in a small mixing bowl. Beat until spreading consistency. Additional sugar may be needed, if frosting is too thin.

Cinnamon Chocolate Chip Drops

Makes approximately 3 dozen.

    3 cups Basic Cookie Mix (Recipe on page 6)
    1 teaspoon cinnamon
    ¼ cup milk
    1 egg, lightly beaten
    1 cup Hershey's Semi-Sweet Chocolate Mini Chips
    ¾ cup chopped nuts

Combine all ingredients, except Mini Chips and nuts, in a large bowl; blend well. Stir in Mini Chips and nuts. Drop by teaspoonfuls onto a greased cookie sheet. Bake at 375° for 10 to 12 minutes. Remove from cookie sheet; cool on a wire rack.

Chocolate Cherry Drops

Makes approximately 4 dozen.

    ½ cup plus 2 tablespoons butter or margarine
    1 cup granulated sugar
    1 egg
    1 teaspoon vanilla
    1¼ cups unsifted all-purpose flour
    ¼ cup plus 2 tablespoons Hershey's Cocoa
    ½ teaspoon baking soda
    ½ teaspoon salt
    1 cup chopped, well-drained maraschino cherries
    ½ cup chopped nuts
      Candied cherries or walnut pieces, optional

Cream butter or margarine and sugar in a large bowl. Add egg and vanilla; blend well. In a separate bowl combine flour, cocoa, baking soda, and salt. Blend flour mixture into creamed mixture. Stir in maraschino cherries and chopped nuts. Drop by rounded teaspoonfuls onto an ungreased cookie sheet. Garnish with candied cherries or walnut pieces, if desired. Bake at 350° for 10 to 12 minutes or until set. Remove from cookie sheet. Cool on a wire rack.

Chocolate Nut Drop Cookies

Makes approximately 2 dozen.

    1 egg
    1 tablespoon vegetable oil
    1 teaspoon vanilla
    2 cups Chocolate Cookie Mix (Recipe on page 12)
    ½ cup chopped nuts
      Maraschino cherries or walnut halves

Combine egg, oil, and vanilla in a bowl; beat until well blended. Add cookie mix and chopped nuts; blend well. Drop by teaspoonfuls onto a lightly greased cookie sheet. Top with a maraschino cherry or walnut half. Bake at 375° for 8 to 10 minutes or until set. Remove from cookie sheet; cool on a wire rack.

Peanut Butter Chip Chocolate Cookies

Makes approximately 5 dozen.

    1 cup butter or margarine
    1½ cups granulated sugar
    2 eggs
    2 teaspoons vanilla
    2 cups unsifted all-purpose flour
    ⅔ cup Hershey's Cocoa
    ¾ teaspoon baking soda
    ½ teaspoon salt
    2 cups (12-ounce package) Reese's Peanut Butter Chips

Cream butter or margarine, sugar, eggs, and vanilla in a large bowl. In a separate bowl combine flour, cocoa, baking soda, and salt. Blend into creamed mixture. Stir in peanut butter chips. Drop by teaspoonfuls onto an ungreased cookie sheet. (Alternate method: Chill until firm enough to handle. Shape into 1-inch balls. Place on an ungreased cookie sheet. Flatten slightly with a fork.) Bake at 350° for 8 to 10 minutes. Cool 1 minute on cookie sheet before removing to a wire rack.

Double Decker Brownies

Makes 16.

    1 recipe Brownies (Recipe on page 12)
    1 cup miniature marshmallows
    1 cup Reese's Peanut Butter Chips
    1 tablespoon shortening
    1½ cups crisp rice cereal

Prepare recipe for Brownies, omitting nuts. Bake for 25 minutes. Remove from oven. Evenly sprinkle miniature marshmallows over brownies. Return to oven. Bake 5 additional minutes. Remove from oven. Cool in pan. Combine peanut butter chips and shortening in the top of a double boiler over hot, *not* boiling, water. Stir until melted. Add the rice cereal; stir until thoroughly coated. Spread over top of marshmallows. Cool until set. Cut into squares.

Cocoa Pinwheel Cookies

Makes approximately 3 dozen.

½ cup butter *or* margarine
1 3-ounce package cream cheese
1 cup granulated sugar
1 egg
1 teaspoon vanilla
1½ cups unsifted all-purpose flour
½ teaspoon baking powder
½ teaspoon salt
⅛ teaspoon baking soda
½ cup Hershey's Cocoa
¾ cup unsifted all-purpose flour

Cream butter *or* margarine, cream cheese, sugar, egg, and vanilla in large bowl. In a separate bowl combine 1½ cups flour, baking powder, salt, and baking soda. Gradually add flour mixture to creamed mixture; blend well. Divide dough in half. Blend cocoa into one half of the dough. Blend ¾ cup flour into remaining dough. Roll each portion into a 9-inch square. (If dough is too soft, chill for 15 minutes.) Place chocolate layer on top of vanilla; roll up jelly-roll style. Wrap tightly in waxed paper or plastic wrap. Chill at least 1 hour or overnight. Slice dough ¼-inch thick. Place on an ungreased cookie sheet. Bake at 350° for 12 to 15 minutes or until lightly browned. Remove from cookie sheet. Cool on a wire rack.

Ornament Cookies

Makes approximately 2 dozen.

½ cup butter *or* margarine
¾ cup granulated sugar
1 egg
¾ teaspoon pure mint *or* peppermint extract
1 tablespoon milk
1½ cups unsifted all-purpose flour
⅓ cup Hershey's Cocoa
½ teaspoon baking powder
⅛ teaspoon salt
Red cinnamon candies, colored sprinkles, gumdrops, optional

Cream butter *or* margarine, sugar, egg, extract, and milk in a large bowl until light and fluffy. In a separate bowl stir together flour, cocoa, baking powder, and salt. Gradually add flour mixture to creamed mixture; blend well. Divide dough into quarters. Wrap tightly; chill 2 to 3 hours. Roll out dough, one-quarter at a time, to ⅛-inch thickness on a lightly floured cloth-covered board. Cut out half of the dough with a gingerbread boy or girl cookie cutter, or use a star, bell, reindeer, Santa Claus, or other Christmas shapes; cut remaining dough into 3 x 2½-inch rectangles to resemble gift tags. Make a hole in the top of each cookie for hanging on the tree. Place cookies 1 inch apart on an ungreased cookie sheet. Use cinnamon candies to make buttons on gingerbread cookies and holly berries on gift tags. Bake at 325° for 8 to 10 minutes or until firm. Remove from cookie sheet; cool on a wire rack. Decorate cookies with Decorator Frosting and, if desired, colored sprinkles and gumdrops.

Decorator Frosting

2½ to 3 cups confectioners' sugar
2 egg whites
¼ teaspoon peppermint extract

Combine all ingredients in a small bowl. Increase speed to high and beat until mixture is very stiff.

Cocoa Press Cookies

Makes approximately 4½ dozen.

1 cup butter *or* margarine
⅔ cup granulated sugar
1 egg
1 teaspoon vanilla
2¼ cups unsifted all-purpose flour
⅓ cup Hershey's Cocoa
½ teaspoon salt

Cream butter *or* margarine, sugar, egg, and vanilla in large bowl. In a separate bowl combine flour, cocoa, and salt. Blend into creamed mixture. Fill cookie press with dough. Press cookies onto a cool, ungreased cookie sheet. Bake at 350° for 5 to 7 minutes or until set. Remove from cookie sheet. Cool on a wire rack.

Peanut Butter Chip Orange Bars

Makes 16.

2 cups Basic Cookie Mix (Recipe on page 6)
½ cup sour cream
2 teaspoons grated orange peel
1 cup Reese's Peanut Butter Chips
1 cup confectioners' sugar
1½ tablespoons orange juice

Combine cookie mix, sour cream, and orange peel in a small bowl. Stir in peanut butter chips. Spread in a greased 9-inch square baking pan. Bake at 350° for 20 to 25 minutes. Combine confectioners' sugar and orange juice; drizzle over cooled mixture. Cut into bars.

Cookies

Deluxe Marbled Brownies

Makes approximately 2 dozen.

1 cup butter *or* margarine, softened
2 cups granulated sugar
4 eggs
2 teaspoons vanilla
1⅓ cups unsifted all-purpose flour
¾ cup Hershey's Cocoa
1 teaspoon baking powder
½ teaspoon salt
1 cup chopped nuts, optional
⅓ cup butter *or* margarine
2 3-ounce packages cream cheese, softened
⅓ cup granulated sugar
2 tablespoons unsifted all-purpose flour
2 eggs
¾ teaspoon vanilla

Cream the 1 cup butter *or* margarine and 2 cups sugar in large bowl. Add 4 eggs, 1 at a time, beating well after each addition. Blend in 2 teaspoons vanilla. In a separate bowl combine 1⅓ cups flour, cocoa, baking powder, and salt. Gradually add flour mixture to creamed mixture; blend well. Stir in nuts, if desired. Spread half of the batter into a greased 13 x 9-inch baking pan.

Cream ⅓ cup butter *or* margarine and cream cheese in small bowl. Add ⅓ cup sugar and 2 tablespoons flour; blend well. Add 2 eggs and ¾ teaspoon vanilla; beat until smooth.

Spread cream cheese mixture over chocolate batter in pan. Carefully spread remaining chocolate batter over cream cheese mixture. Gently swirl with a spatula or knife for marbled effect. Bake at 350° for 40 to 50 minutes or until brownie begins to pull away from edges of pan. Cool in pan. Frost, if desired. Cut into squares.

Chocolate Brownies

Makes 16.

2 eggs
1 cup granulated sugar
½ teaspoon vanilla
½ cup butter *or* margarine, melted
½ cup unsifted all-purpose flour
⅓ cup Hershey's Cocoa
¼ teaspoon baking powder
¼ teaspoon salt
½ cup chopped nuts, optional

Beat eggs in small bowl. Gradually add sugar and vanilla; beat well. Blend in melted butter *or* margarine. In a separate bowl combine flour, cocoa, baking powder, and salt. Gradually blend flour mixture into egg mixture until thoroughly blended. Stir in nuts. Spread in a greased, 8-inch square baking pan. Bake at 350° for 30 to 35 minutes or until brownie begins to pull away from edges of pan. Cool in pan. Frost, if desired. Cut into squares.

Peanut Butter Chip Brownies

Makes 16.

⅓ cup butter *or* margarine
¾ cup granulated sugar
¼ cup light corn syrup
2 teaspoons vanilla
2 eggs
½ cup unsifted all-purpose flour
⅓ cup Hershey's Cocoa
½ teaspoon salt
1 cup Reese's Peanut Butter Chips

Cream butter *or* margarine and sugar in large bowl. Blend in corn syrup and vanilla. Add eggs, 1 at a time, beating well after each addition. In a separate bowl combine flour, cocoa, and salt; gradually add to creamed mixture. Stir in peanut butter chips. Pour into a greased 8-inch square baking pan. Bake at 350° for 30 to 35 minutes or until brownie begins to pull away from edges of pan. Cool in pan. Frost, if desired. Cut into squares.

Honey Brownies

Makes 16.

⅓ cup butter *or* margarine
¾ cup granulated sugar
⅓ cup honey
2 teaspoons vanilla
2 eggs
½ cup unsifted all-purpose flour
⅓ cup Hershey's Cocoa
½ teaspoon salt
1 cup chopped nuts

Cream butter *or* margarine and sugar in a small bowl. Blend in honey and vanilla. Add eggs; beat well. In a separate bowl combine flour, cocoa, and salt. Gradually add to creamed mixture. Stir in nuts. Spread in a greased, 9-inch square baking pan. Bake at 350° for 25 to 30 minutes or until brownie begins to pull away from edges of pan. Cool in pan. Frost, if desired. Cut into squares.

Hi-Protein Energy Bar

Makes 18 bars.

- ½ cup butter or margarine
- 1⅓ cups packed brown sugar
- 2 eggs
- 1 teaspoon vanilla
- ⅓ cup Hershey's Cocoa
- ¼ cup milk
- ¼ cup nonfat dry milk crystals
- ¼ cup wheat germ
- 1 cup unsifted whole wheat flour
- ½ teaspoon baking powder
- ¼ teaspoon baking soda
- 2 cups (12-ounce package) Reese's Peanut Butter Chips
- ½ cup raisins

Cream butter or margarine, sugar, eggs, and vanilla in large bowl until light and fluffy. Blend in cocoa and milk; add dry milk crystals, wheat germ, flour, baking powder, and baking soda. Beat until ingredients are thoroughly combined. Fold in peanut butter chips and raisins. Spread mixture evenly in a greased 13 x 9 x 2-inch baking pan. Bake at 350° for 30 to 35 minutes. Cool in pan on a wire rack. Cut into bars.

Peanut Butter Chip Breakfast Bars

Makes approximately 5 dozen.

- ¼ cup butter or margarine
- ¼ cup shortening
- 1 cup packed light brown sugar
- 1 egg
- 1 teaspoon vanilla
- 1⅓ cups unsifted all-purpose flour
- ½ teaspoon baking soda
- ½ teaspoon salt
- ½ teaspoon ground cinnamon
- ¼ cup milk
- 1⅔ cups granola or natural cereal, crumbled
- 1 cup seedless raisins
- 1 cup flaked coconut
- 2 cups (12-ounce package) Reese's Peanut Butter Chips

Cream butter or margarine, shortening, brown sugar, egg, and vanilla in large bowl. In a separate bowl combine flour, baking soda, salt, and cinnamon. Alternately add flour mixture and milk to creamed mixture. Stir in cereal, raisins, coconut, and peanut butter chips. Spread batter evenly in a foil-lined 15½ x 10½ x 1-inch jelly-roll pan. Bake at 350° for 20 to 25 minutes. Cool completely. Invert pan. Peel off foil. Cut into 1 x 2-inch bars.

Peanut Butter Chip and Jelly Bars

Makes 3 dozen.

- 3 cups unsifted all-purpose flour
- 1 cup granulated sugar
- 1½ teaspoons baking powder
- 1 cup butter or margarine, softened
- 2 eggs, lightly beaten
- 1 cup grape jelly
- 2 cups (12-ounce package) Reese's Peanut Butter Chips

Combine flour, sugar, and baking powder in a large bowl. Cut in butter or margarine until mixture resembles coarse crumbs. Stir in beaten eggs; stir until mixture is smooth. Reserve half of the mixture. Press remaining half of mixture onto the bottom of a greased 13 x 9 x 2-inch baking pan. Spread grape jelly evenly over crust in pan. Sprinkle 1 cup peanut butter chips over jelly. Crumble remaining dough over chips. Bake at 375° for 30 to 35 minutes or until lightly browned. Remove from oven. Immediately sprinkle with remaining 1 cup chips. Cool. Cut into bars.

Cherry-Bright Chocolate Brownies

Makes 16.

- ⅓ cup butter or margarine
- ¾ cup granulated sugar
- 2 eggs
- ¼ cup light corn syrup
- 2 tablespoons kirsch or other cherry liqueur, or
  - 1 teaspoon almond extract
- 1 teaspoon vanilla
- ⅔ cup unsifted all-purpose flour
- ⅓ cup Hershey's Cocoa
- ½ teaspoon salt
- ¼ teaspoon baking powder
- ½ cup chopped, well-drained maraschino cherries
- ⅓ cup chopped, slivered almonds
  - Halved maraschino cherries, optional

Cream butter or margarine, granulated sugar, and eggs in a small bowl. Blend in corn syrup, kirsch or almond extract, and vanilla. In a separate bowl combine flour, cocoa, salt, and baking powder. Gradually add flour mixture to creamed mixture; blend well. Stir in chopped cherries and almonds. Spread in a greased and floured 9-inch square baking pan. Bake at 350° for 25 to 30 minutes or until brownie begins to pull away from edges of pan. Cool in pan. Frost, if desired. Cut into squares. Garnish with additional maraschino cherry halves, if desired.

Pies

Cocoa Chiffon-Cloud Pie

Makes 8 servings.

    1 9-inch baked pastry shell *or* crumb crust, cooled
    1 envelope unflavored gelatin
    ¼ cup cold water
    ½ cup granulated sugar
    ½ cup Hershey's Cocoa
    ½ teaspoon salt
    1¼ cups milk
    3 egg yolks
    1 cup heavy cream
    3 egg whites
       Additional whipped cream, optional

Prepare pie shell; set aside.

Sprinkle gelatin over water in a small bowl; let stand to soften, about 5 minutes. Combine sugar, cocoa, and salt in a small saucepan. Stir in milk and egg yolks. Cook over low heat, stirring constantly, until mixture thickens slightly; do *not* boil. Remove from heat. Add gelatin; stir until dissolved. Chill until syrupy. Whip cream until stiff. Gently fold whipped cream into chocolate mixture. Beat egg whites until stiff, but not dry. Fold egg whites into chocolate mixture. Pour mixture into pie shell. Chill until set. Garnish with additional whipped cream, if desired.

Chocolate Bavarian Cream Pie

Makes 8 servings.

    1 9-inch baked pastry shell *or* crumb crust, cooled
    1¾ cups milk
    1 envelope unflavored gelatin
    ⅔ cup granulated sugar
    6 tablespoons Hershey's Cocoa
    1 tablespoon light corn syrup
    2 tablespoons butter *or* margarine
    ¾ teaspoon vanilla
    1 cup heavy cream

Prepare pie shell; set aside.

Pour 1 cup of the milk into a saucepan. Sprinkle gelatin over milk. Let stand for 5 minutes to soften gelatin. Combine sugar and cocoa; add to mixture in saucepan. Add corn syrup. Cook and stir over medium heat until mixture comes to a boil. Remove from heat. Add butter *or* margarine; stir until melted. Blend in remaining ¾ cup milk and vanilla. Pour into large bowl. Cool to room temperature. Chill until almost set. Whip cream

until stiff. Whip chocolate gelatin on medium speed until smooth. Blend half of the whipped cream into the chocolate on low speed just until smooth. Pour into pie shell. Chill until set. Top with remaining whipped cream.

Chocolate Eggnog Chiffon Pie

Makes 8 servings.

       Chocolate Crumb Crust
    1 envelope unflavored gelatin
    1¼ cups milk
    3 egg yolks, lightly beaten
    ¾ cup granulated sugar, divided
    ¼ teaspoon salt
    1 cup Hershey's Semi-Sweet Chocolate Mini Chips
    3 tablespoons rum *or* 1 teaspoon rum extract
    ¼ teaspoon nutmeg
    3 egg whites
    ½ cup heavy cream
       Additional whipped cream and nutmeg, optional

Prepare crumb crust; set aside to cool.

Sprinkle gelatin over milk in saucepan. Let stand 5 minutes to soften gelatin. Blend in egg yolks, ½ cup of the sugar, and salt. Place over medium heat, stirring constantly, until gelatin dissolves and mixture thickens slightly. Do *not* boil. Remove from heat. Place Mini Chips in a bowl. Add about 1 cup of the gelatin mixture to Mini Chips. Stir until melted. Add remaining gelatin mixture, rum, and nutmeg. Cool to room temperature. Chill until almost set. Remove from refrigerator. Beat 1 minute with mixer until smooth.

Beat egg whites in small bowl until foamy. Gradually add remaining ¼ cup sugar, beating until stiff peaks form. Fold into chocolate mixture.

Whip cream in small bowl until stiff; fold into chocolate mixture. Chill 15 minutes. Mound into pie shell. If desired, garnish with additional whipped cream and sprinkle with nutmeg.

Chocolate Crumb Crust

    1½ cups vanilla wafer crumbs
    6 tablespoons Hershey's Cocoa
    ⅓ cup confectioners' sugar
    6 tablespoons butter *or* margarine, melted

Combine crumbs, cocoa, and sugar in a bowl. Stir in butter *or* margarine. Press mixture onto bottom and sides of a 9-inch pie plate. Bake at 350° for 8 to 10 minutes. Cool.

Chocolate Bavarian Cream Pie, above

Pies

Chocolate-Butterscotch Pie

Makes 8 servings.

 Macaroon-Nut Crust
⅔ cup packed light brown sugar
¼ cup Hershey's Cocoa
3 tablespoons unsifted all-purpose flour
2 tablespoons cornstarch
½ teaspoon salt
2¼ cups milk
½ cup light corn syrup
3 egg yolks, beaten
2 tablespoons butter *or* margarine
1 teaspoon vanilla
 Sweetened whipped cream, optional

Prepare Macaroon-Nut Crust; set aside.

Combine sugar, cocoa, flour, cornstarch, and salt in a medium saucepan. Blend in milk, corn syrup, and egg yolks. Cook over medium heat, stirring constantly, until mixture comes to a boil. Boil and stir for 1 minute. Remove from heat. Blend in butter *or* margarine and vanilla. Pour into cooled pie shell. Carefully press plastic wrap directly onto pie filling. Cool to room temperature. Chill. Serve with sweetened whipped cream, if desired.

Macaroon-Nut Crust

1¼ cups crisp coconut cookie crumbs
½ cup chopped walnuts
¼ cup melted butter *or* margarine

Combine all ingredients in a small bowl; blend well. Press firmly into a 9-inch pie plate. Bake at 350° for 8 to 10 minutes; cool.

Chocolate Swirl Ice Cream Pie

Makes 8 to 10 servings.

 Chocolate Cookie Crust
 Chocolate Sauce
1½ quarts strawberry, peppermint, *or* coffee ice cream, slightly softened
 Sweetened strawberries, optional

Prepare Chocolate Cookie Crust.

Prepare Chocolate Sauce.

Spread about half of the ice cream into the frozen pie shell. Spoon about ½ cup of the Chocolate Sauce over the ice cream. Top with remaining ice cream. Drizzle on ¼ cup of the Chocolate Sauce. Freeze until firm. Cover with plastic wrap or aluminum foil. Serve with remaining Chocolate Sauce. Garnish with sweetened strawberries, if desired.

Chocolate Cookie Crust

1½ cups chocolate wafer cookie crumbs
⅓ cup butter *or* margarine, melted

Combine chocolate cookie crumbs and melted butter *or* margarine in a 9-inch pie plate. Press firmly against the bottom and sides. Bake at 350° for 8 to 10 minutes. Cool; freeze.

Chocolate Sauce

Makes approximately 1 cup.

¼ cup granulated sugar
2 tablespoons unsifted all-purpose flour
2 tablespoons milk
1 egg, well beaten
½ cup (5.5-ounce can) Hershey's Chocolate Flavored Syrup
¼ cup butter *or* margarine
½ teaspoon vanilla

Mix sugar and flour in a small saucepan. Blend in milk, egg, and chocolate syrup. Cook over low heat, stirring constantly, until mixture comes to a boil. Boil and stir 1 minute. Remove from heat. Blend in butter *or* margarine and vanilla. Cool.

Chocolate Peppermint Whirlaway Pie

Makes 8 to 10 servings.

 Graham Cracker Crust (Recipe on page 21)
36 large marshmallows *or* 3½ cups miniature marshmallows
¾ cup milk
1½ teaspoons vanilla
⅛ teaspoon pure mint *or* peppermint extract
 Chocolate Sauce (Recipe above)
⅛ teaspoon red food color
3½ cups (1 8-ounce container) frozen nondairy whipped topping, thawed

Prepare piecrust; set aside. Melt marshmallows with milk in the top of a double boiler over hot, *not* boiling, water; stir until smooth. Cool slightly. Stir in vanilla and extract. Chill, stirring occasionally, until mixture mounds when dropped from a spoon. Prepare Chocolate Sauce; cool. Set aside ½ cup. Fold marshmallow mixture and food color into whipped topping in a small bowl. Alternately layer marshmallow mixture with Chocolate Sauce in crumb crust. Swirl with a rubber spatula to create a marbled effect. Cover; freeze several hours or overnight. Serve with reserved sauce.

Milk Chocolate Pie

Makes 8 servings.

> Graham Cracker Crust
> 1 (½ pound) Hershey's Milk Chocolate Bar
> ¼ cup milk
> 3½ cups (1 8-ounce container) frozen nondairy whipped topping, thawed *or* whipped cream
> Hershey's Semi-Sweet Chocolate Mini Chips

Prepare Graham Cracker Crust; set aside. Break chocolate bar into pieces. Melt chocolate with milk in the top of double boiler over hot, *not* boiling, water. Cool completely. Fold whipped topping *or* whipped cream into cooled chocolate. Pour into crust. Garnish with Mini Chips. Cover; chill several hours until firm. Can also be frozen.

Graham Cracker Crust

> 1¼ cups graham cracker crumbs
> ¼ cup granulated sugar
> ¼ cup butter *or* margarine, melted

Combine crumbs, sugar, and melted butter *or* margarine in a medium bowl. Blend thoroughly with a fork or pastry blender. Press mixture into the bottom and sides of a 9-inch pie plate. Bake at 350° for 8 to 10 minutes. Cool.

Chocolate Peanut Butter Pie

Makes 8 servings.

> Peanut Butter Chip Crust
> 1 cup Reese's Peanut Butter Chips
> 1 cup Hershey's Semi-Sweet Chocolate Mini Chips
> 1 envelope unflavored gelatin
> ½ cup granulated sugar
> 1¾ cups milk
> 2 egg yolks, lightly beaten
> 1 teaspoon vanilla
> 2 egg whites
> 1 tablespoon granulated sugar
> Whipped cream, optional
> Chocolate shavings *or* Reese's Peanut Butter Chips, optional

Prepare Peanut Butter Chip Crust; set aside. Place peanut butter chips into one bowl and Mini Chips into a second bowl; set aside. Combine gelatin and ½ cup sugar in a saucepan. Add milk and egg yolks. Cook over medium heat, stirring constantly, until gelatin is dissolved and mixture lightly coats a spoon. Do *not* boil. Remove from heat. Stir in vanilla. Slowly pour 1 cup of the gelatin mixture into the bowl containing the chocolate; stir until melted. Gradually add remaining hot mixture, ½ cup at a time, to the peanut butter chips; stir until melted. Chill both mixtures until partially set. Pour chocolate into prepared pie shell. Beat egg whites with the 1 tablespoon sugar. Fold egg whites into peanut butter mixture. Pour over chocolate layer. Chill thoroughly before serving. Garnish with whipped cream and chocolate shavings or additional peanut butter chips, if desired.

Peanut Butter Chip Crust

> ¾ cup Reese's Peanut Butter Chips
> 1 cup vanilla wafers *or* graham cracker crumbs
> 2 tablespoons granulated sugar
> 5 tablespoons butter *or* margarine, melted and cooled

Chop peanut butter chips with a nut chopper or blender. Add crushed chips to cookie crumbs and sugar. Drizzle on melted butter *or* margarine. Blend thoroughly. Press mixture into bottom and sides of a 9-inch pie plate. Chill.

Chocolate Amaretto Pie

Makes 8 servings.

> Graham Cracker Crust (Recipe on this page)
> ⅓ cup Hershey's Cocoa
> 1 cup granulated sugar
> ⅓ cup cornstarch
> ¼ teaspoon salt
> 2¾ cups milk
> 3 tablespoons Amaretto
> 2 tablespoons butter *or* margarine
> 1 teaspoon vanilla
> Sliced almonds, optional

Prepare piecrust; set aside.

Combine cocoa, sugar, cornstarch, and salt in a medium saucepan. Gradually blend in milk; stir until smooth. Cook over medium heat, stirring constantly, until mixture comes to a boil; boil and stir 1 minute. Remove from heat. Blend in Amaretto, butter *or* margarine, and vanilla. Pour into piecrust. Chill until firm. Just before serving, pipe on Amaretto Whipped Cream. Garnish with sliced almonds, if desired.

Amaretto Whipped Cream

Makes approximately 1 cup.

> ½ cup heavy cream
> 2 tablespoons confectioners' sugar
> 1 to 2 teaspoons Amaretto

Whip cream, sugar, and Amaretto until stiff.

Pies

Velvety Chocolate Cream Pie

Makes 8 servings.

    1 9-inch baked pastry shell *or* crumb crust, cooled
    ⅓ cup Hershey's Cocoa
    1¼ cups granulated sugar
    ⅓ cup cornstarch
    ¼ teaspoon salt
    3 cups milk
    3 tablespoons butter *or* margarine
    1½ teaspoons vanilla
        Sweetened whipped cream *or* nondairy whipped topping, optional
        Chocolate curls, optional

Prepare pie shell; set aside.

Combine cocoa, sugar, cornstarch, and salt in a medium saucepan. Blend in milk until smooth. Cook and stir over medium heat until mixture comes to a boil. Boil and stir for 3 minutes. Remove from heat. Blend in butter *or* margarine and vanilla. Pour into pie shell. Carefully press plastic wrap directly onto pie filling. Chill 3 to 4 hours. Serve with sweetened whipped cream *or* whipped topping and chocolate curls, if desired.

Variations

Mocha: Add 2 teaspoons dry instant coffee to dry ingredients.

Rum: Omit vanilla. Add 3 to 4 tablespoons light rum.

Chocolate Coconut Cream Pie

Makes 8 servings.

    1 9-inch baked pastry shell *or* crumb crust, cooled
    ⅔ cup granulated sugar
    ⅓ cup cornstarch
    ¼ teaspoon salt
    3 cups milk
    3 egg yolks, lightly beaten
    1 tablespoon butter
    2 teaspoons vanilla
    ½ cup flaked coconut
    3 tablespoons Hershey's Cocoa
    3 tablespoons granulated sugar
    2 tablespoons milk
    3 egg whites
    ¼ teaspoon cream of tartar
    6 tablespoons granulated sugar

Prepare pie shell; set aside.

Combine the ⅔ cup sugar, cornstarch, salt, and 3 cups milk in a medium saucepan. Blend in egg yolks. Stir constantly over medium heat until mixture comes to a boil. Boil and stir for 1 minute. Remove from heat. Stir in butter and vanilla. Pour 1½ cups of the cooked mixture into a small bowl. Stir in coconut. Set aside.

Combine cocoa, the 3 tablespoons sugar, and the 2 tablespoons milk in a small bowl. Blend cocoa mixture into remaining mixture in saucepan. Pour 1 cup of the chocolate mixture into the pie shell. Spread coconut mixture over chocolate. Top with remaining chocolate mixture; spread evenly. Prepare meringue by beating egg whites with cream of tartar until foamy. Gradually add the 6 tablespoons sugar; beat until stiff peaks form. Spread meringue over hot pie filling, carefully sealing to edge of crust. Bake at 350° for 8 to 10 minutes or until lightly browned. Cool to room temperature; chill several hours.

Chocolate Banana Cream Pie

Makes 8 servings.

    1 9-inch baked pastry shell *or* crumb crust, cooled
    2 ounces Hershey's Unsweetened Baking Chocolate
    2½ cups milk
    1 cup granulated sugar
    5 tablespoons cornstarch
    ½ teaspoon salt
    3 egg yolks, lightly beaten
    1 tablespoon butter
    1 teaspoon vanilla
    2 medium bananas, sliced
    1 cup nondairy whipped topping *or* whipped cream, optional

Prepare piecrust; set aside.

Place baking chocolate and 1½ cups of the milk in top of double boiler over simmering water; heat and stir until chocolate is melted. In a separate bowl combine sugar, cornstarch, and salt; blend in remaining 1 cup milk. Gradually add to chocolate mixture, stirring constantly. Immediately add egg yolks. Cook until mixture thickens, stirring constantly. Cook and stir 5 minutes longer. Remove from heat. Add butter and vanilla. Pour into a bowl. Press plastic wrap directly onto filling. Cool. Spread a small amount of filling over the bottom of the pie shell. Arrange a layer of banana slices on top of filling. Spread on remaining filling. Press plastic wrap directly onto filling. Chill. Serve garnished with whipped topping *or* whipped cream, if desired.

Cakes

Glazed Chocolate Torte

Makes 10 to 12 servings.

- ¼ cup shortening
- ¾ cup granulated sugar
- 3 egg yolks
- 1 teaspoon vanilla
- ⅓ cup ground blanched almonds
- 3 ounces Hershey's Unsweetened Baking Chocolate, melted
- 1 cup sifted all-purpose flour
- ½ teaspoon baking powder
- ½ teaspoon baking soda
- ½ teaspoon salt
- ¾ cup milk, at room temperature
- 3 egg whites
- ¼ cup granulated sugar
  Filling
  Glaze

Cream shortening with ¾ cup sugar. Add egg yolks and vanilla; beat well. Stir in almonds, then baking chocolate. In a separate bowl sift together flour, baking powder, baking soda, and salt; add to creamed mixture alternately with milk, blending well after each addition. Beat egg whites until frothy; gradually add ¼ cup sugar and beat until stiff peaks form. Carefully fold into chocolate mixture and turn into two greased and cocoa-dusted 8-inch round cake pans. Bake at 350° for 20 minutes or until cake begins to pull away from edge of pan. Cool 10 minutes; remove from pans and cool on wire racks. When completely cool, split layers horizontally; fill and glaze.

Filling

- 1½ cups heavy cream, sweetened and whipped or
- 3 cups frozen nondairy whipped topping, thawed

Glaze

- 1 ounce Hershey's Unsweetened Baking Chocolate
- 2 tablespoons butter or margarine
- 1 tablespoon light corn syrup
- 1 cup confectioners' sugar
- 2 tablespoons hot water

Combine chocolate, butter or margarine, and corn syrup in top of double boiler over simmering water. Stir in confectioners' sugar and hot water; beat well. While still warm, pour glaze over torte. Spread quickly, allowing glaze to run down the sides. Refrigerate until serving time.

Luscious Chocolate Cake

Makes 10 to 12 servings.

- 4 ounces Hershey's Unsweetened Baking Chocolate
- ⅓ cup butter or margarine
- 1¾ cups unsifted all-purpose flour
- 1½ cups granulated sugar
- 1½ teaspoons baking soda
- 1 teaspoon salt
- 1½ cups sour cream
- 2 eggs
- 1 teaspoon vanilla

Melt baking chocolate and butter or margarine in top of double boiler over hot, not boiling, water; cool. Combine remaining ingredients in large bowl; blend in melted chocolate. Beat 3 minutes at medium speed. Pour into two greased and floured 9-inch round cake pans. Bake at 350° for 30 to 35 minutes or until cake tester inserted comes out clean. Cool 10 minutes; remove from pans. Cool completely on wire racks; frost.

5-Way Chocolate Cake

Makes 8 to 10 servings.

- ½ cup butter or margarine
- ½ cup shortening
- 2¼ cups granulated sugar
- 2 eggs
- 1 teaspoon vanilla
- ⅔ cup Hershey's Cocoa
- 2½ cups unsifted all-purpose flour
- 1½ teaspoons baking soda
- ½ teaspoon baking powder
- 1 teaspoon salt
- 2 cups buttermilk

Cream butter or margarine, shortening, and sugar in a large bowl until light and fluffy. Add eggs and vanilla; beat well. In a separate bowl combine cocoa, flour, baking soda, baking powder, and salt; add alternately with buttermilk to creamed mixture. Pour into well-greased and floured pans. Bake at 350° as follows: three 8-inch round cake pans for 30 to 35 minutes; one 13 x 9 x 2-inch pan for 55 to 65 minutes; one 10-inch tube or Bundt pan for 55 to 65 minutes; two 9 x 5 x 3-inch loaf pans for 50 to 60 minutes. For 3½ dozen cupcakes (2½ inches in diameter), bake 20 to 25 minutes at 375°.

Orange-Kissed Chocolate Cupcakes

Makes 24.

 ¾ cup shortening
1¼ cups granulated sugar
 2 eggs
 1 teaspoon vanilla
1¾ cups unsifted all-purpose flour
 ½ cup Hershey's Cocoa
 1 teaspoon baking soda
 ½ teaspoon salt
 1 cup milk
   Orange or Vanilla Cream Filling
 1 6-ounce package (about 24) Hershey's Milk
   Chocolate Kisses

Cream shortening and sugar in large bowl. Add eggs and vanilla; blend well. In a separate bowl combine flour, cocoa, baking soda, and salt; add alternately with milk to creamed mixture. Fill 24 paper-lined 2½-inch muffin cups two-thirds full with batter. Bake at 375° for 20 to 25 minutes or until cake tester inserted comes out clean. Cool completely.

Prepare Orange or Vanilla Cream Filling. Cut a 1½-inch cone from top of cupcake. Fill cavity with filling; replace cone. Swirl filling over top. Top with *unwrapped* Chocolate Kiss.

Orange Cream Filling

Makes approximately 3 cups.

 ¼ cup unsifted all-purpose flour
 ½ cup milk
 ¼ cup butter or margarine
 ¼ cup shortening
 1 tablespoon finely grated orange peel
 2 teaspoons orange juice
 ¼ teaspoon salt
 4 cups confectioners' sugar
   Red and yellow food color, optional

Combine flour and milk in a small saucepan. Cook, stirring constantly, until mixture thickens and just begins to boil. Remove from heat. Chill thoroughly.

Cream butter or margarine and shortening in large bowl. Add orange peel, orange juice, and salt; blend in chilled flour mixture. Gradually add confectioners' sugar, beating to spreading consistency. Stir in food color, if desired.

Variation

Vanilla Cream Filling: Substitute 2 teaspoons vanilla for orange juice and grated peel. Omit food color.

Cocoa-Lite Angel Food Cake

Makes 12 to 14 servings.

 1 14½-ounce box Angel Food Cake mix
 ⅓ cup Hershey's Cocoa
   Mocha Chiffon Filling

Prepare egg white mixture as directed on package. Pour contents of cake flour mixture into small bowl. Stir cocoa into cake flour mixture until well blended. Blend cocoa-cake flour mixture gradually into beaten egg whites. Mix at low speed and scrape bowl often until dry mix disappears, about 1 minute. Pour batter into two ungreased 9 x 5 x 3-inch loaf pans or a 10-inch tube pan. Cut through batter with knife or spatula to remove large air bubbles. Bake at 375° for 30 to 40 minutes or until top crust is golden brown, firm, and looks dry. Do *not* underbake. Cool in pan, inverted on cooling rack or hanging upside down on funnel or bottle. When completely cool, slice loaf or ring into 3 thin layers horizontally. Spread each layer generously with ¾ cup Mocha Chiffon Filling, reserving ¼ cup for garnish or frosting top.

Mocha Chiffon Filling

Makes 2 cups.

 1 envelope dry whipped topping mix
 ½ cup cold low-fat or skim milk
 1 teaspoon instant coffee granules
 2 teaspoons Hershey's Cocoa
 1 teaspoon vanilla

Combine ingredients in deep, narrow-bottom bowl at low speed until blended. Whip on high speed until soft peaks form. Whip 2 minutes longer or until topping is light and fluffy.

Chocolate Fudge Cake

Makes 10 to 12 servings.

½ cup butter *or* margarine, softened
½ cup shortening
2 cups granulated sugar
2 eggs
1 teaspoon vanilla
2¼ cups unsifted all-purpose flour
½ cup Hershey's Cocoa
1¼ teaspoons baking soda
½ teaspoon salt
1⅓ cups water

Cream butter *or* margarine, shortening, and sugar in large bowl. Add eggs and vanilla; blend thoroughly. In a separate bowl combine flour, cocoa, baking soda, and salt; add alternately with water to creamed mixture. Pour into two greased and floured 9-inch round cake pans or two 8-inch square cake pans. Bake at 350° for 35 to 40 minutes for 9-inch layers; 40 to 45 minutes for 8-inch layers or until cake tester inserted comes out clean. Cool 10 minutes; remove from pans. Cool completely on wire racks; frost.

Chocolate Chiffon Peanut Butter Cake

Makes 10 to 12 servings.

1½ cups unsifted cake flour
1¾ cups granulated sugar
⅔ cup Hershey's Cocoa
2 teaspoons baking powder
½ teaspoon baking soda
1 teaspoon salt
½ cup vegetable oil
7 eggs, separated
¾ cup cold water
2 teaspoons vanilla
½ teaspoon cream of tartar
¼ cup granulated sugar
    Peanut Butter Whipped Cream

Combine flour, 1¾ cups sugar, cocoa, baking powder, baking soda, and salt in a large bowl. Make a well in mixture; add oil, egg yolks, water, and vanilla. Beat with a wooden spoon until smooth.

Beat egg whites and cream of tartar in large bowl until frothy; gradually add ¼ cup sugar and beat until stiff peaks form.

Gradually pour chocolate batter over beaten egg whites, gently folding just until blended. Pour

into ungreased 10-inch tube pan. Bake at 325° for 1 hour and 20 to 30 minutes or until done (cake springs back when lightly touched). Invert cake over funnel or bottle until completely cool. Loosen cake with spatula. Invert on serving plate. Prepare Peanut Butter Whipped Cream; frost. Garnish as desired.

Peanut Butter Whipped Cream

1 cup Reese's Peanut Butter Chips
⅓ cup milk
1½ cups miniature marshmallows *or*
    15 large marshmallows
1 cup heavy cream
½ teaspoon vanilla

Place peanut butter chips, milk, and marshmallows in top of double boiler over simmering water. Stir until marshmallows and chips are completely melted; cool to lukewarm. Whip heavy cream until stiff; fold in vanilla and peanut butter mixture.

Red Velvet Cocoa Cake

Makes 10 to 12 servings.

½ cup butter *or* margarine
1½ cups granulated sugar
1 teaspoon vanilla
2 eggs
1 tablespoon red food color
2 cups unsifted all-purpose flour
¼ cup Hershey's Cocoa
1 teaspoon salt
1 cup buttermilk *or* sour milk*
1½ teaspoons baking soda
1 tablespoon vinegar
    Fluffy Vanilla Frosting (See recipe on page 37)

Cream butter *or* margarine, sugar, and vanilla in large bowl. Add eggs and food color; blend thoroughly. In separate bowl combine flour, cocoa, and salt; add alternately with buttermilk *or* sour milk to creamed mixture. Stir baking soda into vinegar; fold carefully into batter (do *not* beat). Pour into two greased and floured 9-inch round cake pans. Bake at 350° for 30 to 35 minutes or until cake tester inserted comes out clean. Cool 10 minutes; remove from pans. Cool completely on wire racks; frost with Fluffy Vanilla Frosting.

To Sour Milk: Use 1 tablespoon vinegar plus milk to equal 1 cup.

Cakes

Mini Chip Petits Fours

Makes approximately 5½ dozen.

⅔ cup butter *or* margarine
1⅓ cups granulated sugar
1 teaspoon vanilla
2 eggs
2 cups unsifted all-purpose flour
1¼ teaspoons baking powder
¼ teaspoon salt
⅔ cup milk
1 cup Hershey's Semi-Sweet Chocolate Mini Chips
Chocolate Petits Fours Glaze

Line a 15½ x 10½ x 1-inch jelly-roll pan with aluminum foil; grease foil.

Cream butter *or* margarine, sugar, and vanilla in large bowl until light and fluffy. Add eggs, beating well. In a separate bowl combine flour, baking powder, and salt; add alternately with milk to creamed mixture, beating just until smooth. Stir in Mini Chips. Pour batter into prepared pan. Bake at 350° for 20 to 25 minutes or until cake tester inserted comes out clean. Cool 10 minutes; remove from pan. Remove foil; cool completely. Cut cake into hearts, diamonds, circles, or squares (approximately 1½-inch shapes). Place cake pieces on a wire rack with waxed paper or cookie sheet below to catch drips. Cover until ready to glaze.

Prepare Chocolate Petits Fours Glaze. Frost by spooning chocolate glaze over cake pieces so entire piece is covered. Allow glaze to set. Decorate with Mini Chips and/or candied fruit pieces, or pipe decorations with tubes of glossy decorating gels or frosting.

Note: Cake can also be baked in a greased and floured 9 x 5 x 3-inch loaf pan at 350° for 55 to 60 minutes. Cover with Chocolate Petits Fours Glaze and garnish with Mini Chips.

Chocolate Petits Fours Glaze

⅓ cup granulated sugar
3 tablespoons water
1 cup Hershey's Semi-Sweet Chocolate Mini Chips
3 tablespoons marshmallow creme
1 to 2 tablespoons hot water

Combine sugar and 3 tablespoons water in a small saucepan; bring to a boil. Remove from heat and immediately add Mini Chips; stir until melted. Blend in marshmallow creme and enough hot water until glaze is of pouring consistency. Remelt the drippings over hot water as additional glaze is needed.

Sour Cream Chocolate Cake

Makes 10 to 12 servings.

3 ounces Hershey's Unsweetened Baking Chocolate
½ cup butter *or* margarine
1 cup boiling water
2 cups packed light brown sugar
2 cups unsifted all-purpose flour
1½ teaspoons baking soda
1 teaspoon salt
2 eggs
½ cup sour cream
1 teaspoon vanilla

Combine baking chocolate, butter *or* margarine, and boiling water in a small bowl; stir until chocolate and butter *or* margarine are melted. Combine brown sugar, flour, baking soda, and salt in large bowl. Gradually add chocolate mixture; blend well. Add eggs, sour cream, and vanilla; beat one minute at medium speed. Pour into a greased and floured 13 x 9 x 2-inch pan. Bake at 350° for 35 minutes or until cake tester inserted comes out clean.

Vermont Cocoa Cake

Makes 10 to 12 servings.

½ cup Hershey's Cocoa
½ cup boiling water
¼ cup butter *or* margarine
¼ cup shortening
2 cups granulated sugar
⅛ teaspoon salt
1 teaspoon vanilla
2 eggs
1½ teaspoons baking soda
1 cup buttermilk *or* sour milk*
1¾ cups unsifted all-purpose flour
3 tablespoons buttermilk *or* sour milk**
1 teaspoon imitation maple flavor
⅓ cup chopped walnuts

Stir together cocoa and boiling water in small bowl until smooth; set aside. Cream butter *or* margarine, shortening, sugar, salt, and vanilla in a large bowl. Add eggs; beat well. Stir baking soda into 1 cup buttermilk *or* sour milk; add alternately with flour to creamed mixture.

Measure 1⅔ cups batter into a small bowl. Stir in 3 tablespoons buttermilk *or* sour milk, maple flavor, and nuts; pour into a greased and waxed paper-lined 8- or 9-inch layer pan. Blend cocoa mixture into remaining batter; pour into two greased and waxed paper-lined 8- or 9-inch round cake pans. Bake at 350° for 30 to 35 minutes for 8-inch layers; 25 to 30 minutes for 9-inch layers or until cake tester inserted comes out clean. Cool 5 minutes; remove from pans. Cool completely on wire racks. Fill and frost, placing Maple-Nut layer between cocoa layers.

Variation

Orange-Nut: Stir ⅛ teaspoon baking soda into the 3 tablespoons buttermilk *or* sour milk before adding to 1⅔ cups batter. Substitute ½ to ¾ teaspoon grated orange peel for maple flavor. Prepare recipe as above.

To Sour Milk: Use 1 tablespoon vinegar plus milk to equal 1 cup.

**To Sour Milk:* Use ½ teaspoon vinegar plus milk to equal 3 tablespoons.

Chocolate Syrup Swirl Cake

Makes 12 to 14 servings.

    1 cup butter *or* margarine
    2 cups granulated sugar
    3 eggs
    2 teaspoons vanilla
 2¾ cups unsifted all-purpose flour
    1 teaspoon baking soda
    ½ teaspoon salt
    1 cup buttermilk *or* sour milk*
    1 cup Hershey's Chocolate Flavored Syrup
    ¼ teaspoon baking soda
    1 cup flaked coconut, optional
      Mini Chip-Marshmallow Glaze (See recipe
      on page 37)

Cream butter *or* margarine and sugar in large bowl; blend in eggs and vanilla. In a separate bowl combine flour, 1 teaspoon baking soda, and salt; add alternately with buttermilk *or* sour milk to creamed mixture. Combine chocolate syrup and ¼ teaspoon baking soda; blend into 2 cups batter. Add coconut, if desired, to remaining batter and pour into a greased and floured 12-cup Bundt pan or 10-inch tube pan. Pour chocolate batter over vanilla batter in pan; do *not* mix. Bake at 350° about 1 hour and 10 minutes. Cool 15 minutes; remove from pan. Cool completely on wire rack; drizzle with Mini Chip-Marshmallow Glaze.

To Sour Milk: Use 1 tablespoon vinegar plus milk to equal 1 cup.

Cocoa Snowballs

Makes 30.

    3 eggs
 1½ cups granulated sugar
    ½ cup Hershey's Cocoa
    ¾ cup milk
    ¼ cup butter *or* margarine
    1 teaspoon vanilla
    ½ teaspoon salt
 1½ cups unsifted all-purpose flour
    ½ teaspoon baking soda
    2 7.2-ounce packages fluffy white frosting mix
 2⅔ cups flaked coconut

Beat eggs until thick and lemon colored in a small bowl. Gradually beat in ½ cup sugar. Combine remaining 1 cup sugar and cocoa in saucepan. Add milk and butter *or* margarine; cook and stir constantly until sugar is dissolved and butter *or* margarine is melted. Remove from heat; add vanilla and salt. Pour egg mixture into a large bowl. In a separate bowl combine flour and baking soda; fold alternately with chocolate mixture into egg mixture just until blended. Fill 30 paper-lined 2½-inch muffin cups about one-half full with batter. Bake at 325° for 20 to 25 minutes or until cake tester inserted comes out clean. Cool completely. Prepare frosting mix according to package directions. Remove cupcake papers. Frost top, bottom, and sides of each cupcake; roll in coconut. Let stand at room temperature until frosting is firm.

Chocolatetown Syrup Cupcakes

Makes approximately 30.

    ½ cup butter *or* margarine
    1 cup granulated sugar
    1 teaspoon vanilla
    4 eggs
 1¼ cups unsifted all-purpose flour
    ¾ teaspoon baking soda
 1½ cups (1-pound can) Hershey's Chocolate
      Flavored Syrup

Cream butter *or* margarine, sugar, and vanilla in large bowl until light and fluffy. Add eggs; beat well. In a separate bowl combine flour and baking soda; add alternately with chocolate syrup to creamed mixture. Fill paper-lined 2½-inch muffin cups one-half full with batter. Bake at 375° for 15 to 20 minutes. Cool; frost as desired.

Holiday Chocolate Cake

Makes 10 to 12 servings.

2 cups granulated sugar
1¾ cups unsifted all-purpose flour
¾ cup Hershey's Cocoa
2 teaspoons baking soda
1 teaspoon baking powder
1 teaspoon salt
2 eggs
1 cup buttermilk *or* sour milk*
1 cup strong black coffee *or* 2 teaspoons instant coffee dissolved in 1 cup hot water
½ cup vegetable oil
2 teaspoons vanilla
Ricotta Cheese Filling
Chocolate Whipped Cream Frosting

Combine sugar, flour, cocoa, baking soda, baking powder, and salt in large bowl. Add eggs, buttermilk *or* sour milk, coffee, oil, and vanilla; beat at medium speed for 2 minutes (batter will be thin). Pour into two greased and floured 9-inch round cake pans. Bake at 350° for 30 to 35 minutes or until cake tester inserted comes out clean. Cool 10 minutes; remove from pans. Cool completely on wire racks. Slice cake layers in half horizontally. Place bottom slice on serving plate; top with one-third of Ricotta Cheese Filling. Alternate cake layers and filling ending with cake on top. Frost with Chocolate Whipped Cream.

To Sour Milk: Use 1 tablespoon vinegar plus milk to equal 1 cup.

Ricotta Cheese Filling

1¾ cups (15 ounces) ricotta cheese*
¼ cup granulated sugar
3 tablespoons Grand Marnier *or* orange-flavored liqueur *or* orange juice concentrate, undiluted
¼ cup candied red *or* green cherries, coarsely chopped
⅓ cup Hershey's Semi-Sweet Chocolate Mini Chips

Combine ricotta cheese, sugar, and liqueur in small bowl; beat until smooth. Fold in candied fruit and Mini Chips.

*If ricotta cheese is unavailable, substitute 1 cup heavy cream. Whip with sugar and liqueur until stiff.

Chocolate Whipped Cream

Makes approximately 2½ cups.

⅓ cup confectioners' sugar
2 tablespoons Hershey's Cocoa
1 cup heavy cream
1 teaspoon vanilla

Combine confectioners' sugar and cocoa in small bowl. Add cream and vanilla; beat until stiff.

Orange-Frosted Cocoa Bundt Cake

Makes 12 to 14 servings.

¾ cup butter *or* margarine
1⅔ cups granulated sugar
2 eggs
1 teaspoon vanilla
¾ cup sour cream
2 cups unsifted all-purpose flour
⅔ cup Hershey's Cocoa
½ teaspoon salt
2 teaspoons baking soda
1 cup buttermilk *or* sour milk*
Orange *or* Vanilla Frosting

Cream butter *or* margarine, sugar, eggs, and vanilla in large bowl; blend in sour cream. In a separate bowl combine flour, cocoa, and salt. Stir baking soda into buttermilk *or* sour milk; add alternately with dry ingredients to creamed mixture. Beat 2 minutes at medium speed. Pour batter into greased and floured 9-cup or 12-cup Bundt pan. Bake at 350° for 45 to 50 minutes or until cake tester inserted comes out clean. Cool 10 minutes; remove from pan. Cool completely on a wire rack. Frost with Orange *or* Vanilla Frosting.

Orange Frosting

1 cup confectioners' sugar
2 tablespoons butter *or* margarine, melted
1½ tablespoons orange juice
½ teaspoon vanilla
¼ teaspoon grated orange peel

Combine all ingredients in small bowl; beat until smooth.

Variation

Vanilla Frosting: Substitute 1½ tablespoons water for orange juice and omit orange peel. Prepare as above.

To Sour Milk: Use 1 tablespoon vinegar plus milk to equal 1 cup.

Cakes

Cocoa Cake Roll

Makes 10 to 12 servings.

  3 egg yolks
½ cup granulated sugar
½ cup unsifted all-purpose flour
⅓ cup Hershey's Cocoa
⅓ cup granulated sugar
½ teaspoon baking soda
¼ teaspoon salt
⅓ cup water
  1 teaspoon vanilla
  3 egg whites
  1 tablespoon granulated sugar
    Peanut Butter Whipped Cream Filling
    Chocolate Glaze

Line a 15½ x 10½ x 1-inch jelly-roll pan with aluminum foil; grease foil generously. Beat egg yolks in a small bowl on high speed about 3 minutes; gradually add ½ cup sugar. Continue beating for 2 minutes. In a separate bowl combine flour, cocoa, ⅓ cup sugar, baking soda, and salt; add alternately with water and vanilla on low speed just until batter is smooth. Beat egg whites until foamy; add 1 tablespoon sugar and beat until stiff peaks form. Carefully fold beaten egg whites into chocolate mixture. Spread batter evenly into prepared pan. Bake at 375° for 15 to 18 minutes or until top springs back when touched lightly. Invert onto slightly dampened towel; carefully remove foil. Immediately roll cake and towel together from narrow end. Let stand 1 minute. Unroll and remove towel; reroll cake. Cool completely on a wire rack. Prepare Peanut Butter Whipped Cream Filling.

Unroll cake and spread with filling; reroll. Garnish with additional whipped cream and Chocolate Glaze. Chill about 1 hour before serving.

Peanut Butter Whipped Cream Filling

  1 cup Reese's Peanut Butter Chips
⅓ cup milk
1½ cups miniature marshmallows or
    15 large marshmallows
  1 cup heavy cream
½ teaspoon vanilla

Place peanut butter chips, milk, and marshmallows in top of double boiler over simmering water. Stir until marshmallows and chips are completely melted; cool to lukewarm. Whip heavy cream until stiff; fold in vanilla and peanut butter mixture.

Chocolate Glaze

  2 tablespoons butter or margarine
  2 tablespoons Hershey's Cocoa
  2 tablespoons water
  1 cup confectioners' sugar
½ teaspoon vanilla

Melt butter or margarine in a small saucepan over low heat; add cocoa and water, stirring constantly, until mixture thickens. Do not boil. Remove from heat; cool slightly. (Cool completely for a thicker, frosting-type topping.) Blend in confectioners' sugar and vanilla.

Chocolate Marble Cake

Makes 12 to 14 servings.

2½ cups unsifted all-purpose flour
1¾ cups granulated sugar
  1 teaspoon baking soda
  2 teaspoons baking powder
½ teaspoon salt
⅓ cup shortening
⅓ cup butter or margarine, softened
  3 eggs
1⅔ cups buttermilk or sour milk*
1½ teaspoons vanilla
⅓ cup Hershey's Cocoa
⅓ cup granulated sugar
¼ teaspoon baking soda
¼ cup water
    Chocolate Glaze (See recipe on page 37)

Combine flour, 1¾ cups sugar, 1 teaspoon baking soda, baking powder, and salt in large bowl. Add shortening, butter or margarine, eggs, buttermilk or sour milk, and vanilla; beat on medium speed for 3 minutes. Combine cocoa, ⅓ cup sugar, and ¼ teaspoon baking soda in a small bowl; blend in water and ⅔ cup of vanilla batter. Pour vanilla batter into greased and floured 9-cup Bundt pan or two 9 x 5 x 3-inch loaf pans. Spoon cocoa batter on top; swirl with spatula or knife for marbled effect. Bake at 375° for 50 to 55 minutes for Bundt pan; 325° for 60 to 65 minutes for loaf pans or until cake tester inserted comes out clean. Cool 1 hour; remove from pan. Cool completely on a wire rack. Prepare Chocolate Glaze; spoon warm glaze onto cake.

*To Sour Milk: Use 1 tablespoon plus 2 teaspoons vinegar plus milk to equal 1⅔ cups.

Hershey's Sweet Chocolate Cake
Makes 12 servings.

- 1 4-ounce bar Hershey's Sweet Baking Chocolate
- 1/3 cup water
- 1/2 cup butter *or* margarine, softened
- 1 cup granulated sugar
- 1 teaspoon vanilla
- 3 egg yolks
- 1 2/3 cups unsifted all-purpose flour
- 1 teaspoon baking soda
- 1/2 teaspoon salt
- 2/3 cup buttermilk *or* sour milk*
- 3 egg whites, stiffly beaten
  Coconut-Pecan Frosting *or* Seven-Minute Frosting (Recipe on page 37)

Break chocolate bar into small pieces; add to water in a small saucepan. Stir over low heat until chocolate is melted. Remove from heat; cool to room temperature. Cream butter *or* margarine, sugar, and vanilla in large bowl. Add egg yolks, one at a time, beating well after each addition. Blend in chocolate. In a separate bowl combine flour, baking soda, and salt; add alternately with buttermilk *or* sour milk to creamed mixture, beating after each addition until smooth. Fold in beaten egg whites. Pour into two greased and floured 9-inch round cake pans. Bake at 350° for 30 to 35 minutes or until cake tester inserted comes out clean. Cool 10 minutes; remove from pans. Cool completely on wire racks; fill and frost top with Coconut-Pecan Frosting *or* Seven-Minute Frosting.

Coconut-Pecan Frosting

- 2/3 cup evaporated milk
- 2/3 cup granulated sugar
- 1/4 cup butter *or* margarine
- 1 egg, lightly beaten
- 1 cup coconut
- 1/2 cup chopped pecans
- 1/2 teaspoon vanilla

Combine evaporated milk, sugar, butter *or* margarine, and egg in a saucepan. Cook and stir over medium heat until thickened and bubbly, about 12 minutes. Add coconut, pecans, and vanilla. Cool until thick enough to spread, beating occasionally.

To Sour Milk: Use 2 teaspoons vinegar plus milk to equal 2/3 cup.

Chocolate Pound Cake
Makes 12 to 14 servings.

- 1 1/2 cups butter, softened
- 3 cups granulated sugar
- 2 teaspoons vanilla
- 5 eggs
- 2 teaspoons instant coffee granules
- 1/4 cup hot water
- 2 cups unsifted all-purpose flour
- 3/4 cup Hershey's Cocoa
- 1 teaspoon salt
- 1/2 teaspoon baking powder
- 1 cup buttermilk *or* sour milk*

Cream butter, sugar, and vanilla in large bowl for 5 minutes at medium speed. Add eggs, one at a time, beating well after each addition. Dissolve coffee granules in water. In a separate bowl combine flour, cocoa, salt, and baking powder; add alternately with coffee and buttermilk *or* sour milk to creamed mixture, beating just until mixture is blended. Pour into greased and floured 12-cup Bundt pan or 10-inch tube pan. Bake at 325° for 1 hour and 20 minutes, or until cake tester inserted comes out clean. Cool 20 minutes; remove from pan. Cool completely; sprinkle with confectioners' sugar.

To Sour Milk: Use 1 tablespoon vinegar plus milk to equal 1 cup.

Lickity-Split Cocoa Cake
Makes 6 to 8 servings.

- 1 1/2 cups unsifted all-purpose flour
- 1 cup granulated sugar
- 1/4 cup Hershey's Cocoa
- 1 teaspoon baking soda
- 1/2 teaspoon salt
- 1 cup water
- 1/4 cup plus 2 tablespoons vegetable oil
- 1 tablespoon vinegar
- 1 teaspoon vanilla

Combine flour, sugar, cocoa, baking soda, and salt in a large bowl. Add water, oil, vinegar, and vanilla; stir until smooth and thoroughly blended. Pour into a greased and floured 9-inch round cake pan or 8-inch square baking pan. Bake at 350° for 35 to 40 minutes or until cake tester inserted comes out clean. Cool 10 minutes; remove from pan. Cool completely on wire rack; frost.

Frostings & Sauces

Classic Chocolate Sauce

Makes approximately 2 cups.

- ¼ cup plus 2 tablespoons Hershey's Cocoa
- 1 cup granulated sugar
- ¾ cup evaporated milk
- ¼ cup butter *or* margarine
- ⅛ teaspoon salt
- ½ teaspoon vanilla

Combine cocoa and sugar in a small saucepan. Blend in evaporated milk. Add butter *or* margarine and salt. Cook, stirring constantly, until mixture just begins to boil. Remove from heat. Stir in vanilla. Serve warm over ice cream, pie, or other desserts.

Peanut Butter Chip Ice Cream Sauce

Makes approximately 1 cup.

- 1 cup Reese's Peanut Butter Chips
- ¼ cup evaporated milk
- 2 tablespoons light corn syrup
- 1 tablespoon butter
- 1 teaspoon vanilla

Place all ingredients, except vanilla, in a small, heavy saucepan. Stir constantly over low heat until chips and butter are melted and mixture is smooth. Remove from heat. Stir in vanilla. Serve warm over ice cream.

Chocolate Sauce

Makes approximately 2 cups.

- 1 cup granulated sugar
- ½ cup light corn syrup
- 1 egg, well beaten
- 2 ounces Hershey's Unsweetened Baking Chocolate
- ⅔ cup evaporated milk
- 1 teaspoon vanilla

Combine sugar, corn syrup, and egg in a medium saucepan. Add chocolate. Cook over medium heat, stirring constantly, until mixture comes to a full boil. Boil and stir for 3 minutes. Remove from heat. Let stand for 5 minutes. Gradually stir in evaporated milk and vanilla. Serve over cake or ice cream.

Easy Chocolate Bar Fondue

Makes approximately 1 cup.

- 1 (½ pound) Hershey's Milk Chocolate Bar
- ⅓ cup light cream *or* evaporated milk
- Fondue Dippers (See below)

Break chocolate bar into pieces. Place chocolate in a fondue pot or in the top of a double boiler. Add light cream *or* evaporated milk. Stir over low heat until chocolate is melted. Serve warm with a selection of Fondue Dippers.

Mt. Gretna Chocolate Fondue

Makes approximately 2 cups.

- 3½ ounces Hershey's Unsweetened Baking Chocolate
- 1⅓ cups (14-ounce can) sweetened condensed milk
- ¼ cup marshmallow creme
- 1 tablespoon milk
- 1½ teaspoons vanilla
- 1 tablespoon creamy peanut butter, optional
- Fondue Dippers

Combine baking chocolate and sweetened condensed milk in a heavy saucepan or in the top of a double boiler. Stir constantly over low heat until chocolate is melted and mixture is smooth. Blend in marshmallow creme and milk. Just before serving, stir in vanilla and, if desired, peanut butter. Transfer to a fondue pot. Serve warm with a selection of Fondue Dippers.

Fondue Dippers

- Nut halves
- Marshmallows
- Pieces of cake (angel food, sponge, or pound)
- Ladyfingers
- Fresh fruit (strawberries, pineapple chunks, mandarin orange segments, cherries, sliced apples, pears, peaches, or bananas)

Before making fondue, select your choice of the listed dippers.

Fresh fruit should be well drained and brushed with lemon juice to prevent browning.

Frostings & Sauces

Burnt Sugar Frosting

Makes approximately 4 cups.

- ¾ cup granulated sugar
- ¾ cup boiling water
- ¾ cup butter *or* margarine
- 2 egg yolks
- 6 cups confectioners' sugar

Pour sugar into a large, heavy skillet. Heat slowly, stirring occasionally, until sugar melts and starts to turn a dark golden color. Very gradually add water, stirring constantly. Continue cooking until sugar dissolves. Boil 2 minutes. Set aside to cool completely.

Cream butter *or* margarine in large bowl until smooth. Add egg yolks; blend thoroughly. Add sugar syrup and confectioners' sugar to creamed mixture; beat until smooth.

Cocoa Mint Frosting

Makes approximately 2¼ cups.

- ½ cup butter *or* margarine
- ½ cup Hershey's Cocoa
- 3⅔ cups (1-pound box) confectioners' sugar
- ⅓ cup milk
- ½ teaspoon pure mint *or* peppermint extract

Melt butter *or* margarine over low heat in a small saucepan. Add cocoa. Heat, stirring constantly, until mixture just begins to boil. Remove from heat. Pour into small bowl. Alternately add confectioners' sugar and milk. Beat to spreading consistency. Blend in mint *or* peppermint extract. Spread frosting while still warm.

Creamy Chocolate Frosting

Makes approximately 3 cups.

- 3 tablespoons butter *or* margarine
- 3 ounces Hershey's Unsweetened Baking Chocolate
- ¼ teaspoon salt
- ½ cup milk
- 3 cups confectioners' sugar
- 1 teaspoon vanilla

Melt butter *or* margarine in a small saucepan. Add chocolate. Stir constantly over very low heat until chocolate melts and mixture is smooth. Pour into small bowl. Stir in salt. Alternately add milk and sugar; beat until thoroughly blended. Stir in vanilla. Chill until spreading consistency, about 10 to 15 minutes.

Peanut Butter Chip Frosting

Makes approximately 2 cups.

- ½ cup butter *or* margarine
- ⅓ cup milk
- 1½ cups Reese's Peanut Butter Chips
- 2 cups confectioners' sugar
- 1 teaspoon vanilla

Place butter *or* margarine, milk, and peanut butter chips in a small saucepan. Stir constantly over low heat until chips are melted and mixture is smooth. Remove from heat. Immediately add mixture to confectioners' sugar and vanilla in small bowl; beat until smooth. Spread while frosting is still warm.

Dark Chocolate Butter Cream Frosting

Makes approximately 2 cups.

- 2⅔ cups confectioners' sugar
- ¾ cup Hershey's Cocoa
- 6 tablespoons butter *or* margarine
- 5 to 6 tablespoons milk
- 1 teaspoon vanilla

Combine confectioners' sugar and cocoa in a small bowl. Cream butter *or* margarine with ½ cup of the cocoa mixture in a small bowl. Alternately add remaining cocoa mixture and milk; beat to spreading consistency. Stir in vanilla. For glossier frosting, stir in 1 tablespoon corn syrup.

Light Butter Cream Chocolate Frosting

Makes approximately 2 cups.

- 2⅔ cups confectioners' sugar
- ¼ cup Hershey's Cocoa
- 6 tablespoons butter *or* margarine
- 5 to 6 tablespoons milk
- 1 teaspoon vanilla

Combine confectioners' sugar and cocoa in a small bowl. Cream butter *or* margarine with ½ cup of the cocoa mixture in a small bowl; alternately add remaining cocoa mixture and milk; beat to spreading consistency. Stir in vanilla. For a glossier frosting, stir in 1 tablespoon corn syrup.

Fluffy Vanilla Frosting

Makes approximately 3 cups.

- ½ cup butter *or* shortening
- 5 cups confectioners' sugar
- 2 teaspoons vanilla
- ⅛ teaspoon salt, optional
- 4 to 5 tablespoons milk

Cream butter *or* shortening, 1 cup of the confectioners' sugar, vanilla, and salt in large bowl. Alternately add remaining confectioners' sugar and milk; beat to spreading consistency.

Mini Chip-Marshmallow Glaze

Makes approximately 1 cup.

- ⅓ cup granulated sugar
- 3 tablespoons water
- 1 cup Hershey's Semi-Sweet Chocolate Mini Chips
- 3 tablespoons marshmallow creme
- 1 to 2 tablespoons hot water

Combine sugar and the 3 tablespoons water in a small saucepan. Bring to a boil. Remove from heat. Immediately add Mini Chips; stir until melted. Blend in marshmallow creme. Add hot water, 1 teaspoon at a time, stirring until glaze is desired consistency.

Chocolate Glaze

Makes approximately 1 cup.

- ¼ cup Hershey's Cocoa
- 3 tablespoons water
- 1 tablespoon light corn syrup
- 2 tablespoons butter *or* margarine
- ½ teaspoon vanilla
- 1 cup confectioners' sugar

Combine cocoa, water, corn syrup, and butter *or* margarine in a small saucepan. Stir over low heat until mixture thickens. Remove from heat. Stir in vanilla. Gradually add confectioners' sugar; beat until smooth and thickened.

Fudge Frosting

Makes approximately 1 cup.

- 3 tablespoons butter *or* margarine
- ⅓ cup Hershey's Cocoa
- ½ teaspoon vanilla
- 1⅓ cups confectioners' sugar
- 2 to 3 tablespoons milk

Melt butter *or* margarine in a small saucepan. Add cocoa. Cook over low heat, stirring constantly, until mixture begins to boil. Pour into a small bowl; cool completely. Stir in vanilla. Alternately add confectioners' sugar and milk; beat to spreading consistency.

Quick Chocolate Frosting

Makes approximately 2 cups.

- 4 ounces Hershey's Unsweetened Baking Chocolate
- ¼ cup butter *or* margarine
- 3 cups confectioners' sugar
- 1 teaspoon vanilla
- ⅛ teaspoon salt
- ⅓ cup milk

Combine baking chocolate and butter *or* margarine in a small saucepan; melt chocolate over low heat. Pour into a small bowl. Add confectioners' sugar, vanilla, and salt. Blend in milk; beat to spreading consistency. (If frosting is too thick, add a small amount of milk.)

Brownie Frosting

Makes approximately 1 cup.

- 2 ounces Hershey's Unsweetened Baking Chocolate
- 2 tablespoons butter *or* margarine
- 1¾ cups confectioners' sugar
- ⅛ teaspoon salt
- 3 to 4 tablespoons water
- ½ teaspoon vanilla

Melt baking chocolate and butter *or* margarine in a small saucepan over low heat. Combine confectioners' sugar and salt in small bowl. Gradually add chocolate mixture. Add water, a little at a time. Beat until spreading consistency. Stir in vanilla.

Seven-Minute Frosting

Makes approximately 3 cups.

- 2 egg whites
- 1½ cups granulated sugar
- ⅓ cup water
- 1½ teaspoons vanilla

Combine egg whites, sugar, and water in the top of a double boiler over boiling water. Beat at high speed until frosting holds its shape, about 7 minutes. Remove from heat. Beat in vanilla.

Breads

Peanutty Cocoa Bread

Makes 1 loaf.

- ⅓ cup butter *or* margarine, softened
- 1 cup granulated sugar
- 3 eggs
- 2¼ cups unsifted all-purpose flour
- ⅓ cup Hershey's Cocoa
- 2 teaspoons baking powder
- 1 teaspoon cinnamon
- 1 teaspoon nutmeg
- ½ teaspoon baking soda
- ¼ teaspoon salt
- ¾ cup milk
- 1 cup Reese's Peanut Butter Chips

Cream butter *or* margarine, sugar, and eggs in large bowl. In a separate bowl combine flour, cocoa, baking powder, cinnamon, nutmeg, baking soda, and salt; add alternately with milk to creamed mixture until well blended. Stir in peanut butter chips. Pour batter into a well-greased 9 x 5 x 3-inch loaf pan; bake at 350° for 60 to 65 minutes or until cake tester inserted comes out clean. Remove from pan; cool on a wire rack. Serve with cream cheese *or* butter, if desired.

Cocoa Almond-Filled Braid

Makes 8 to 10 servings.

- Ricotta Cheese Filling
- ½ cup milk
- 1 tablespoon water
- 2 tablespoons butter *or* margarine
- 2¼ to 2½ cups unsifted all-purpose flour
- ¼ cup granulated sugar
- ½ teaspoon salt
- 1 envelope active dry yeast
- 1 egg
- 1 tablespoon margarine, melted
- Vanilla Glaze
- Sliced almonds, optional

Prepare Ricotta Cheese Filling; set aside to chill.

Heat milk, water, and butter *or* margarine over low heat until very warm (120 to 130°F); butter *or* margarine does not need to melt. Stir together 1 cup flour, sugar, salt, and yeast in large bowl; add warm milk mixture and beat at medium speed 2 minutes. Add egg and 1 cup flour; stir by hand until smooth. Sprinkle ¼ cup flour onto kneading surface. Knead dough, adding additional flour as needed, until soft, smooth, and elastic, about 5 minutes. Shape into ball. Place in greased bowl, turning to grease top; allow to rise, covered, in warm place until doubled in bulk, about 1 hour. Roll dough on lightly floured surface into a rectangle measuring 12 by 15 inches; place rectangle onto a lightly greased cookie sheet. Spread filling in center third of rectangle up to ¾-inch of top and bottom edges; make eight diagonal cuts on each side of filling to within 1 inch of filling. Braid strips around filling; pinch ends to seal. Cover; allow to rise in warm place until almost doubled, about 1 hour. Bake at 350° for 30 to 35 minutes or until golden brown; remove from sheet. Brush with melted margarine; allow to cool 20 minutes. Drizzle with Vanilla Glaze; garnish with sliced almonds, if desired. Serve warm or cool.

Ricotta Cheese Filling

- ¾ cup granulated sugar
- ½ cup ricotta cheese
- ½ cup unsifted all-purpose flour
- ¼ cup Hershey's Cocoa
- ½ teaspoon vanilla
- ½ teaspoon almond extract
- ½ cup slivered almonds

Combine sugar, ricotta cheese, flour, cocoa, vanilla, and almond extract in medium bowl; stir in almonds. Chill.

Vanilla Glaze

Blend ½ cup confectioners' sugar and 1 tablespoon milk until smooth.

Peanut Butter-Banana Muffins

Makes approximately 15.

- 1½ cups unsifted all-purpose flour
- ½ cup granulated sugar
- 2 teaspoons baking powder
- ½ teaspoon salt
- 1 egg, lightly beaten
- ½ cup milk
- ¼ cup vegetable oil
- ¾ cup mashed banana
- ¾ cup Reese's Peanut Butter Chips
- ½ cup chopped pecans

Combine flour, sugar, baking powder, and salt in large bowl. Add egg, milk, oil, and mashed banana; stir just until combined. Add peanut butter chips and pecans. Fill paper-lined 2½-inch muffin cups two-thirds full with batter. Bake at 400° for 20 to 25 minutes. Serve warm.

Breads

Apple Surprise Muffins

Makes 12.

- 1½ cups (about 2 medium) peeled, cored, and finely chopped apples
- ½ teaspoon cinnamon
- 1 tablespoon granulated sugar
- ¼ cup chopped nuts
- ¼ cup butter *or* margarine, melted
- ¼ cup Hershey's Cocoa
- ¾ cup applesauce
- 1¼ cups unsifted all-purpose flour
- ½ cup granulated sugar
- ¾ teaspoon baking soda
- ¼ teaspoon salt
- 1 egg, lightly beaten

Combine apples, cinnamon, 1 tablespoon sugar, and nuts in a bowl; blend well. In a separate bowl combine melted butter *or* margarine and cocoa; add applesauce. Combine flour, ½ cup sugar, baking soda, and salt in a bowl; stir in cocoa mixture and egg just until moistened. Place 1 tablespoon batter in each of 12 paper-lined 2½-inch muffin cups; spoon 1 heaping tablespoon apple mixture into each cup, pressing into batter. Top each cup with 1 tablespoon batter. Bake at 375° for 20 minutes or until cake tester comes out clean. Remove from pan; cool.

Pumpkin Bread

Makes 3 loaves.

- 2 cups cooked *or* canned pumpkin
- 1 cup vegetable oil
- ⅔ cup water
- 4 eggs
- 3½ cups unsifted all-purpose flour
- 3 cups granulated sugar
- 2 teaspoons baking soda
- 1½ teaspoons salt
- 1 teaspoon cinnamon
- 2 cups (12-ounce package) Reese's Peanut Butter Chips
- 1 cup chopped nuts
- 1 cup raisins, optional

Blend pumpkin, oil, water, and eggs in large bowl. In a separate bowl combine flour, sugar, baking soda, salt, and cinnamon; gradually add to pumpkin mixture; blend well. Stir in peanut butter chips, nuts, and raisins. Pour into 3 greased and floured 8½ x 4½ x 2½-inch loaf pans. Bake at 350° for 50 to 60 minutes or until cake tester inserted comes out clean. Cool 10 minutes; remove from pans. Cool completely.

Sticky Buns

Makes 16.

- 1 13¾-ounce package hot roll mix
- ½ cup butter *or* margarine
- 1 cup packed brown sugar
- ½ cup light corn syrup
- 1 cup Reese's Peanut Butter Chips
- 2 tablespoons butter *or* margarine, melted
- ½ cup chopped pecans
- ½ cup Reese's Peanut Butter Chips
- ½ cup packed brown sugar
- 1½ tablespoons grated orange peel
- 1 teaspoon cinnamon

Prepare hot roll mix according to package directions. Cover; let rise in warm place until doubled in size. Melt ½ cup butter *or* margarine in a small saucepan; stir in 1 cup brown sugar and corn syrup. Heat and stir until sugar is dissolved; pour into 2 greased 8-inch round pans. Sprinkle each pan with ½ cup peanut butter chips. Roll dough on floured surface to a 14 x 9-inch rectangle; brush dough with 2 tablespoons melted butter *or* margarine. Combine pecans, ½ cup peanut butter chips, ½ cup brown sugar, orange peel, and cinnamon; sprinkle on dough. Roll up dough, jelly-roll fashion, starting with 14-inch side; seal edges. Cut into 16 slices; place in pans, cut sides down. Cover; let rise in warm place until doubled in size. Bake at 350° for 20 to 25 minutes, until golden brown. Invert immediately on a plate.

Mini Chip Swirl Buns

Makes 11.

- 1 envelope active dry yeast
- ¼ cup warm water
- ⅔ cup buttermilk
- 1 egg
- 1¼ cups unsifted all-purpose flour
- ¼ cup butter *or* margarine, softened
- ¼ cup granulated sugar
- 1 teaspoon baking powder
- 1 teaspoon salt
- 1¾ to 2 cups unsifted all-purpose flour

Dissolve yeast in warm water (105 to 115°F).

Combine yeast mixture, buttermilk, egg, 1¼ cups flour, butter *or* margarine, sugar, baking powder, and salt in a large bowl; blend on low speed of mixer. Beat at medium speed for 2 minutes. Stir in 1¾ to 2 cups flour until dough is slightly sticky but easy to handle. Turn dough onto well-floured board; knead for 5 minutes. Roll dough into 16 x 9-inch rectangle.

Prepare Filling; spread evenly over rectangle. Sprinkle with Mini Chips. Roll up dough, jelly-roll fashion, beginning with long side; pinch edges to seal roll. Cut into pieces about 1½ inches wide. Place pieces, cut sides up, on a greased baking sheet in circular fashion, edges touching. Cover; let rise until doubled, about 1 hour. Bake at 350° for 25 to 30 minutes or until golden brown (cover outer edges with foil for last 10 minutes of baking to avoid over-browning). Glaze, if desired. Serve warm.

Filling

- ½ cup packed brown sugar
- 3 tablespoons butter *or* margarine, melted
- ¾ cup chopped nuts
- ¾ cup Hershey's Semi-Sweet Chocolate Mini Chips

Combine brown sugar, butter *or* margarine, and chopped nuts.

Mini Chip Harvest Muffins

Makes approximately 18.

- 1 cup unsifted whole wheat flour*
- 1 cup unsifted all-purpose flour
- 2 teaspoons baking powder
- 1½ teaspoons cinnamon
- 1½ teaspoons nutmeg
- 1 teaspoon salt
- 2 eggs
- ¾ cup milk
- ¼ cup vegetable oil
- ⅓ cup honey
- 2 teaspoons vanilla
- 2 cups grated carrot, apple, *or* zucchini, well drained
- ¾ cup Hershey's Semi-Sweet Chocolate Mini Chips
- ½ cup chopped pecans
  Honey Butter

Combine flours, baking powder, cinnamon, nutmeg, and salt in a large bowl. Beat eggs, milk, oil, honey, and vanilla in a small bowl; add to dry ingredients, stirring just until moistened. Gently stir in carrot, apple, *or* zucchini, Mini Chips, and pecans. Fill paper-lined 2½-inch muffin cups two-thirds full with batter. Bake at 375° for 20 to 25 minutes or until cake tester inserted comes out clean. Serve with Honey Butter.

Honey Butter

Cream ½ cup softened butter until fluffy. Add ¼ cup honey and beat until well blended.

*All-purpose flour may be substituted for whole wheat flour.

Chocolate-Peanut Butter Tea Cake

Makes 1 loaf.

- ¼ cup butter *or* margarine, softened
- ⅔ cup granulated sugar
- 1 egg
- 1 teaspoon vanilla
- 1½ cups unsifted all-purpose flour
- ½ cup Hershey's Cocoa
- 1 teaspoon baking soda
- ½ teaspoon salt
- 1 cup buttermilk
- 2 cups (12-ounce package) Reese's Peanut Butter Chips
- ¼ cup milk

Cream butter *or* margarine in a large bowl until fluffy; beat in sugar, egg, and vanilla. In a separate bowl combine flour, cocoa, baking soda, and salt. Mix in cocoa mixture alternately with buttermilk beginning and ending with dry ingredients, mixing only until ingredients are blended. Stir in 1½ cups of the peanut butter chips. Pour mixture into a greased and floured 9 x 5 x 3-inch loaf pan. Bake at 350° for 60 to 65 minutes or until cake tester inserted comes out clean. Cool on a wire rack 10 minutes; remove from pan and cool thoroughly. Heat remaining ½ cup peanut butter chips and milk in a small saucepan over low heat, stirring frequently, until melted. Drizzle melted chip mixture over warm cake.

Easy Peanut Butter and Jelly Coffeecake

Makes approximately 9 servings.

- 2 cups buttermilk biscuit baking mix
- 2 tablespoons granulated sugar
- 1 egg
- ⅔ cup milk
- 2 tablespoons vegetable oil
- 1½ cups Reese's Peanut Butter Chips
- ½ cup jelly *or* preserves

Combine buttermilk baking mix, sugar, egg, milk, and oil in large bowl; beat until smooth, about ½ minute. Stir in 1 cup of the peanut butter chips. Spread batter into a greased 9-inch square pan; bake at 400° for 20 to 25 minutes or until cake tester inserted comes out clean. Remove from oven; spread immediately with jelly *or* preserves. Sprinkle the remaining ½ cup peanut butter chips over top. Serve warm or cool.

Candies

Chocolate Seafoam

Makes 3 to 4 dozen.

1 ounce Hershey's Unsweetened Baking Chocolate
2 cups packed light brown sugar
¾ cup cold water
½ cup (5½-ounce can) Hershey's Chocolate
  Flavored Syrup
2 egg whites
1 teaspoon vanilla
½ cup broken nuts

Melt baking chocolate in top of double boiler over hot, *not* boiling, water. Combine sugar, water, and chocolate syrup in a heavy 3-quart saucepan. Cook over medium heat, stirring constantly, until sugar dissolves and mixture boils. Continue cooking, without stirring, to 250°F (hard-ball stage) or until small amount of syrup dropped into very cold water forms a ball which is hard enough to hold its shape, yet plastic; remove from heat. Immediately beat egg whites until stiff. Pour hot syrup in a thin stream over beaten egg whites, beating constantly at high speed. Continue beating until mixture forms peaks when dropped from spoon, about 10 minutes. Quickly stir in vanilla and melted baking chocolate by hand. Blend in nuts. Drop by teaspoonfuls onto waxed paper. Cool.

Fudge Caramels

Makes approximately 6 dozen.

3 cups granulated sugar
½ cup Hershey's Cocoa
⅔ cup light corn syrup
1 cup light cream *or* evaporated milk
1 cup milk
1 cup butter *or* margarine
2 tablespoons vanilla

Line bottom and sides of a 9-inch square baking pan with aluminum foil; lightly butter foil.

Combine thoroughly sugar and cocoa in a heavy 4-quart saucepan; blend in corn syrup, cream *or* evaporated milk, milk, and butter *or* margarine. Cook over medium heat, stirring constantly, until sugar dissolves and mixture boils. Cook, stirring occasionally, to 240°F (soft-ball stage) or until small amount of syrup dropped into very cold water forms a soft ball which flattens on removal from water. Reduce heat to low. Continue to cook, stirring constantly, until mixture

reaches 245°F (firm-ball stage) or until small amount of syrup dropped into very cold water forms a firm ball which does not flatten on removal from water. Remove from heat; stir in vanilla. Pour into pan; let cool several hours or overnight. Invert pan; remove aluminum foil. Cut into 1-inch squares with buttered scissors; wrap individually.

Chocolate Mint Squares

Makes approximately 4 dozen.

6 tablespoons sweet butter
½ cup Hershey's Cocoa
2 cups confectioners' sugar
3 tablespoons milk
1 teaspoon vanilla
  Mint Filling

Melt butter in a small saucepan over medium heat; add cocoa. Heat, stirring constantly, just until mixture begins to boil. Remove from heat; add confectioners' sugar, milk, and vanilla. Return to low heat; stir until mixture appears melted and glossy. Pour half onto lightly greased cookie sheet. Quickly spread into 9-inch square with spatula. Chill while preparing Mint Filling. Spread mint evenly over chocolate layer. Chill 10 minutes. Place remaining chocolate over low heat until melted. Quickly spread over filling. Chill thoroughly; cut into small squares.

Mint Filling

1 3-ounce package cream cheese
2 cups confectioners' sugar
½ teaspoon vanilla
¼ teaspoon pure mint *or* peppermint extract
2 or 3 drops green food color
1 tablespoon milk, optional

Combine cream cheese, confectioners' sugar, vanilla, pure mint *or* peppermint extract, and food color; blend well. If needed, add milk, 1 teaspoon at a time, until filling is of spreading consistency.

Variation

Party Patties: Omit chocolate square procedure. Place chocolate mixture in pastry tube. Form 1-inch patties on waxed paper-covered tray; chill until firm. Prepare Mint Filling; spread small amount onto one chocolate patty; top with another patty.

Chocolate Seafoam, above
Fudge Peanut Blossoms, 44
Chocolate Mint Squares, above

Candies

Chocolate Bon Bons

Makes approximately 4 dozen.

⅓ cup butter *or* margarine, softened
¼ cup heavy cream
1½ teaspoons vanilla
3 cups confectioners' sugar
3 ounces Hershey's Unsweetened Baking
Chocolate, melted

Combine butter *or* margarine and heavy cream in small bowl; add vanilla. Gradually add confectioners' sugar and baking chocolate; blend thoroughly. Shape fondant into 1-inch balls and place on waxed paper-covered tray. Cover; chill. Remove from refrigerator 20 minutes before dipping.

Variations

Divide fondant into 3 parts. Add ⅓ cup flaked coconut to first part, ⅛ teaspoon pure mint *or* peppermint extract to second part, and ¼ teaspoon rum extract to third part. Shape into balls and chill.

Chocolate Chip Coating

Makes coating for approximately 5 dozen centers.

1 cup (6-ounce package) Hershey's Semi-Sweet
Chocolate Chips
1 cup (5¾-ounce package) Hershey's Milk
Chocolate Chips
1 tablespoon shortening

To Temper Chocolate: Melt chocolate chips and shortening in a straight-sided bowl set in pan of very warm water. (Temperature of water should *not* be above 120°F). Heat chocolate to 108°F (*not* over 110°F), stirring constantly with rubber spatula; scrape down sides and bottom of bowl frequently so chocolate is evenly and uniformly heated. When chocolate reaches 108°F, remove bowl from pan of water and stir frequently until chocolate cools to 85°F. Continue stirring and scraping bowl constantly until chocolate cools to 80°F. Keep at 80°F for 10 minutes, stirring constantly to develop a shiny gloss. Rewarm cooled chocolate to 86°F over a pan of warm water; hold at 86°F for 5 minutes before dipping. Maintain temperature while dipping. (If temperature exceeds 86°F, retemper by cooling to 80°F.) Centers must be removed from refrigerator and allowed to reach room temperature before coating. (Dipping chilled centers may result in cracked coating and/or bloom on the coating.) Immerse room temperature centers in melted chocolate one at a time; remove with a fork. Gently tap fork on side of pan to remove excess chocolate. Invert candy onto waxed paper-covered tray. Chill coated candies a maximum of 15 minutes in refrigerator to help coating harden. Remove promptly or bloom may occur. Store coated candies at room temperature (60 to 75°F), but keep them well covered.

Butter Cream Centers

Makes approximately 5 dozen.

1 3-ounce package cream cheese, softened
½ cup butter *or* margarine, softened
4 cups unsifted confectioners' sugar
1½ teaspoons vanilla

Beat cream cheese and butter *or* margarine in large bowl until smooth. Blend in confectioners' sugar and vanilla. (If necessary, chill until mixture is firm enough to handle.) Shape into 1-inch balls; place on waxed paper-covered tray or baking sheet. Cover loosely; chill 3 to 4 hours or overnight. Centers should feel dry to touch before coating. Remove from refrigerator about 20 minutes before coating.

Variations

Divide mixture into three parts. Add ⅔ cup flaked coconut to first part, ¼ teaspoon pure mint *or* peppermint extract and 3 drops red *or* green food color to second part, and ¼ teaspoon rum extract to third part.

Fudge Peanut Blossoms

Makes approximately 4 dozen.

2 cups (12-ounce package) Reese's Peanut Butter
Chips
1⅓ cups (14-ounce can) sweetened condensed milk
½ teaspoon orange extract, optional
Chopped nuts *or* granulated sugar
1 9-ounce package (about 54) Hershey's Milk
Chocolate Kisses

Combine peanut butter chips and sweetened condensed milk in top of double boiler over warm water. Heat, stirring occasionally, until chips are melted and mixture is smooth. Stir in orange extract, if desired. Pour into buttered 9-inch square baking pan; cool. Shape into 1-inch balls; roll in chopped nuts *or* sugar. Press *unwrapped* Kiss into center of each ball. Store in airtight container; do *not* refrigerate.

Easy Semi-Sweet Chocolate Coating

Makes coating for approximately 5 dozen centers.

1½ cups Hershey's Semi-Sweet Chocolate Mini Chips
2 tablespoons shortening

Cover cookie sheet or tray with waxed paper; fasten with tape. Chop ½ teaspoon Mini Chips into tiny pieces; set aside. Place remaining Mini Chips and shortening in a 2-cup glass measuring cup or 1½-cup wide-mouth jar. Place measuring cup or jar in pan of warm, *not* hot, water that covers bottom half of measuring cup or jar.

(Do *not* let any water mix with chocolate! If this happens, the chocolate will thicken and tighten and cannot be used for coating.) If necessary, keep pan over low heat, but do *not* allow the water temperature to exceed 125°F.

Stir constantly until chocolate is completely melted and smooth. Remove measuring cup from water; continue stirring until chocolate is cooled to 88°F. (Measuring cup should feel slightly warm to touch.) Stir finely chopped pieces of Mini Chips into melted chocolate until completely blended. (Note: *This is a vital part of procedure and cannot be omitted.* This unmelted chocolate "seeds" the coating and develops the crystals necessary for gloss.) Keeping chocolate between 84 and 86°F, dip *room temperature* centers completely into chocolate, one at a time, with fondue fork, table fork, or hat pin. Gently tap fork or hat pin on side of measuring cup to remove excess chocolate. Invert candy on waxed paper-covered cookie sheet; decorate top of coated center with small amount of melted chocolate, using tip of fork or hat pin. (To keep chocolate between 84 and 86°F while dipping, place measuring cup in warm water.)

Easy Double Peanut Clusters

Makes approximately 2 dozen.

2 cups (12-ounce package) Reese's Peanut Butter Chips
1 tablespoon shortening
2 cups salted peanuts

Melt chips and shortening in top of double boiler over hot, *not* boiling, water. Stir in peanuts. Drop by teaspoonfuls onto waxed paper-lined cookie sheet. Cool until set; store tightly covered.

Peanutty Rocky Road

Makes 64 1-inch squares.

2 cups (12-ounce package) Hershey's Semi-Sweet Chocolate Mini Chips
1 cup (5¾-ounce package) Hershey's Milk Chocolate Chips
1⅓ cups (14-ounce can) sweetened condensed milk
1½ teaspoons vanilla
Dash salt
2 cups (12-ounce package) Reese's Peanut Butter Chips
1½ cups miniature marshmallows

Melt Mini Chips and chocolate chips in top of double boiler over hot, *not* boiling, water; remove from heat. Stir in sweetened condensed milk, vanilla, and salt; blend well. Fold in peanut butter chips and marshmallows. Immediately spread mixture evenly in a foil-lined 8-inch square baking pan. Chill 2 hours or until firm. Invert onto cutting board; remove foil and cut into squares.

Hershey's Cocoa Fudge

Makes 3 dozen squares.

⅔ cup Hershey's Cocoa
3 cups granulated sugar
⅛ teaspoon salt
1½ cups milk
¼ cup butter *or* margarine
1 teaspoon vanilla

Thoroughly combine cocoa, sugar, and salt in a heavy 4-quart saucepan; stir in milk. Bring to rolling boil over medium heat, stirring constantly. Boil without stirring to 234°F (soft-ball stage) or until a small amount of mixture dropped into very cold water forms a soft ball which flattens on removal from water. (Bulb of candy thermometer should not rest on bottom of saucepan.) Remove from heat; add butter *or* margarine and vanilla. *Do not stir.* Cool at room temperature to 110°F; beat until fudge thickens and loses some of its gloss. Quickly spread in a lightly buttered 8- or 9-inch square baking pan; cool.

Variation

Marshmallow-Nut: Increase cocoa to ¾ cup. Cook fudge as above. Add 1 cup marshmallow creme with butter *or* margarine and vanilla. *Do not stir.* Cool to 110°F. Beat 10 minutes; stir in 1 cup broken nuts and pour into pan. (Fudge does not set until poured into pan.)

No-Bake Chocolate-Cherry Mini-Tarts

Makes 30.

  Unbaked Tart Shells
1 3-ounce package cream cheese, softened
2 cups confectioners' sugar
1 teaspoon vanilla
¼ teaspoon almond extract
½ cup coarsely chopped blanched almonds
¼ cup candied cherries, quartered
  Candied cherry halves, optional

Prepare Tart Shells; set aside.

Beat cream cheese in small bowl. Gradually blend in confectioners' sugar, vanilla, and almond extract until smooth. Stir in almonds and cherries. Spoon filling into Tart Shells. Garnish with candied cherry halves, if desired. Chill until firm.

Unbaked Tart Shells

2 cups confectioners' sugar
1 cup vanilla wafer crumbs
1 cup ground almonds
½ cup Hershey's Cocoa
¼ cup milk

Combine confectioners' sugar, wafer crumbs, ground almonds, and cocoa in a bowl. Sprinkle in milk, mixing until ingredients are moistened and cling together. Shape into walnut-size pieces. Place in 30 paper-lined 1¾-inch muffin cups. Press dough against bottom and sides of each cup. Chill.

Chocolate Cheese Cups

Makes 12.

  Graham Crumb Cups
2 ounces Hershey's Unsweetened Baking Chocolate
1 8-ounce package cream cheese, softened
⅔ cup granulated sugar
2 teaspoons vanilla
½ cup sour cream
2 tablespoons granulated sugar

Prepare Graham Crumb Cups; chill.

Melt chocolate in the top of a double boiler over hot, *not* boiling, water. Remove from heat; cool. Beat cream cheese in small bowl until fluffy. Add the ⅔ cup sugar and 1 teaspoon of the vanilla; blend well. Pour in melted chocolate; beat until smooth. Spoon about 2 tablespoons into each Graham Crumb Cup. Chill until set. Combine sour cream, the 2 tablespoons sugar, and remaining 1 teaspoon vanilla. Spread about 2 teaspoons onto top of each cup. Garnish with fresh fruit, if desired.

Graham Crumb Cups

¾ cup graham cracker crumbs
2 tablespoons granulated sugar
3 tablespoons butter *or* margarine, melted

Combine all ingredients in a small bowl; mix well. Pat a small amount on the bottom and partially up the sides of twelve paper-lined 2½-inch muffin cups.

Double-Decker Espresso Mousse

Makes 10 to 12 servings.

1¼ cups granulated sugar
⅓ cup Hershey's Cocoa
2 envelopes unflavored gelatin
2 cups cold espresso*
2 eggs, separated
1 teaspoon vanilla
1 8-ounce package cream cheese, softened
1 cup heavy cream
  Additional whipped cream
  Slivered orange peel, optional
  Chocolate curls, optional

Combine 1 cup of the sugar, cocoa, gelatin, and espresso in a saucepan. Beat egg yolks lightly; add to cocoa mixture. Cook over medium heat, stirring occasionally, until gelatin is dissolved and mixture is slightly thickened. Remove from heat. Stir in vanilla. Cool to room temperature. Whip cream cheese in large bowl. Add gelatin mixture; blend thoroughly. Beat egg whites until foamy. Add remaining ¼ cup sugar, 1 tablespoon at a time, beating until soft peaks form. Beat heavy cream. Fold egg whites and whipped cream into gelatin mixture. Pour into a 1½-quart serving bowl. Cover; chill several hours or overnight.

Unmold and serve with mounds of whipped cream spooned around the edge of the mousse. If desired, sprinkle with orange slivers and chocolate curls.

*Espresso was made by combining 2 tablespoons instant espresso coffee and 2 cups cold water.

Desserts

Rich Chocolate Bar Cheesecake

Makes 10 to 12 servings.

      Almond Crust
    1 (½ pound) Hershey's Milk Chocolate Bar
    4 3-ounce packages cream cheese, softened
    ¾ cup granulated sugar
    2 tablespoons Hershey's Cocoa
      Dash salt
    2 eggs
    ½ teaspoon vanilla
      Sour Cream Topping
      Apricot halves, optional
      Chopped almonds, optional

Prepare Almond Crust; set aside.

Melt milk chocolate bar in the top of a double boiler over warm water. Beat cream cheese in large bowl until light and fluffy. In a small bowl combine sugar, cocoa, and salt. Add cocoa mixture to cream cheese. Beat in eggs and vanilla. Add melted chocolate bar; beat until just blended. Do *not* overbeat. Pour into prepared crust. Bake at 325° for 40 minutes. Turn oven off but do *not* open door. Cool in oven for 30 minutes. Remove from oven. Chill thoroughly. Serve with Sour Cream Topping. If desired, garnish with apricot halves and chopped almonds.

Almond Crust

    ¾ cup graham cracker crumbs
    ⅔ cup chopped slivered almonds
    2 tablespoons granulated sugar
    ¼ cup butter *or* margarine, melted

Combine all ingredients in a small bowl; mix well.

Sour Cream Topping

    ½ cup sour cream
    2 tablespoons granulated sugar
    ½ teaspoon vanilla

Combine all ingredients; blend thoroughly.

Peanut Butter and Banana Pudding Dessert

Makes 4 servings.

    ⅓ cup granulated sugar
    2 tablespoons cornstarch
    2 cups milk
    2 egg yolks, lightly beaten
    1½ cups Reese's Peanut Butter Chips
    2 tablespoons banana-flavored liqueur, optional
    2 to 3 medium-size bananas, sliced ¼-inch thick
    ½ cup Reese's Peanut Butter Chips

Combine sugar and cornstarch in a 2-quart saucepan. Gradually stir in milk and egg yolks. Cook over medium heat, stirring constantly, until mixture comes to a boil. Boil and stir 1 minute. Remove from heat. Add the 1½ cups peanut butter chips; stir until chips are melted and smooth. Stir in banana liqueur. Pour into a bowl. Press plastic wrap directly onto the surface of the pudding. Cool to room temperature. Chill thoroughly. Place ¼ cup pudding in each of four individual dishes. Serve with a layer of banana slices and 2 tablespoons peanut butter chips on top of each dish of pudding.

Dieter's Chocolate Cheesecake

Makes approximately 8 servings.

    ¼ cup skim milk
    1 envelope unflavored gelatin
    ⅔ cup skim milk
    2 egg yolks
    3 tablespoons Hershey's Cocoa
    ¼ cup granulated sugar *or* sugar substitute equivalent
    1½ teaspoons vanilla
    1½ cups (12-ounce carton) small curd creamed cottage cheese
    2 egg whites
    2 tablespoons granulated sugar
    ⅓ cup graham cracker crumbs
    ⅛ teaspoon cinnamon
      Fresh *or* naturally sweetened canned fruit

Pour the ¼ cup milk into blender container. Add gelatin; let stand to soften gelatin while assembling remaining ingredients.

Heat the ⅔ cup milk to boiling. Pour milk into blender; process until gelatin dissolves. Add egg yolks, cocoa, ¼ cup sugar, and vanilla. Process at medium speed until well blended. Add cottage cheese; blend at high speed until smooth. Pour mixture into bowl. Chill until mixture mounds when dropped from a spoon.

Beat egg whites until frothy. Gradually add the 2 tablespoons sugar; beat until stiff peaks form. Fold into chocolate mixture. Combine graham cracker crumbs and cinnamon. Sprinkle crumbs onto the bottom of an 8-inch springform or cake pan. Pour chocolate mixture into pan. Cover and chill several hours or overnight. Arrange fruit on top. Garnish with additional graham cracker crumbs, if desired.

Peanutty Chocolate Pastries

Makes approximately 30.

Filling

- ⅔ cup granulated sugar
- ⅓ cup Hershey's Cocoa
- ½ cup milk
- 2 cups (12-ounce package) Reese's Peanut Butter Chips
- 1 teaspoon vanilla
- ½ cup chopped peanuts, optional

Combine sugar and cocoa in a saucepan. Blend in milk. Add peanut butter chips. Stir over low heat until chips are melted. Stir in vanilla and peanuts. Chill 20 minutes or until mixture is set.

Pastry

- 2 11-ounce packages piecrust mix
- ¼ cup granulated sugar
- ½ cup water
- Milk

Combine piecrust mix, sugar, and water in a bowl. Mix thoroughly until pastry holds together. Shape into a smooth ball. Roll out about a quarter of the dough at a time on a floured pastry cloth to ⅛-inch thickness. Use a 3-inch cookie cutter to cut out fifteen circles from each portion of dough. Place half of the circles on an ungreased cookie sheet. Moisten the edges with milk. Place 1 heaping teaspoon of the Filling in the center of each. Cover with a second circle; stretch circle slightly to meet bottom edges. Press edges together with fingers or fork tines. Brush tops with milk. Bake at 375° for 15 to 20 minutes or until lightly browned.

Nutty Crust Chocolate Cream

Makes 8 to 10 servings.

- 2 ounces Hershey's Unsweetened Baking Chocolate
- ¼ cup water
- 1 envelope unflavored gelatin
- ¾ cup granulated sugar
- ¼ teaspoon salt
- 1½ cups milk
- 4 egg yolks, lightly beaten
- 1 teaspoon vanilla
- 1 cup heavy cream
- Zwieback Crumb Crust

Melt chocolate with water in the top of a double boiler over hot water. In a small bowl combine gelatin, sugar, and salt; let stand to soften gelatin, about 5 minutes. Add to melted chocolate; blend well. Scald milk; add to chocolate mixture. Cook over hot water, stirring occasionally, until gelatin is dissolved, about 5 minutes. Blend a small amount of the hot mixture into the beaten egg yolks. Return to mixture in the double boiler. Cook for 2 minutes, stirring constantly. Remove from heat. Stir in vanilla. Press plastic wrap directly onto filling. Cool to room temperature. Chill until partially set.

Prepare crumb crust.

Whip cream until stiff. Fold into chocolate mixture. Pour into prepared crust. Chill until firm. At serving time, loosen edges with a knife. Invert onto a serving plate. Garnish as desired. Cut into wedges.

Zwieback Crumb Crust

- ¾ cup zwieback crumbs (about 10 slices)
- ⅔ cup finely chopped pecans
- ¼ cup butter or margarine, melted

Line the bottom of an 8-inch round cake pan with waxed paper. Combine crumbs, nuts, and melted butter or margarine; blend thoroughly. Press mixture into bottom and sides of cake pan. Chill.

Chocolate-Orange Mousse

Makes 6 servings.

- 1 cup evaporated milk
- 4 ounces Hershey's Sweet Baking Chocolate
- 1 envelope unflavored gelatin
- ⅔ cup water
- 2 eggs, separated
- ½ teaspoon grated orange rind
- ½ teaspoon vanilla
- ⅓ cup granulated sugar

Combine evaporated milk and chocolate in a medium saucepan. Place over low heat, stirring constantly, until chocolate is melted. Combine gelatin and water in a small bowl; let stand to soften gelatin, about 5 minutes. Add to chocolate mixture in saucepan; stir until gelatin is dissolved. Cool 5 minutes. Beat in egg yolks, 1 at a time. Stir in orange rind and vanilla. Chill until mixture mounds when dropped from a spoon.

Beat egg whites until foamy; gradually add sugar, 2 tablespoons at a time, beating until meringue is stiff but not dry. Fold meringue into chocolate mixture. Spoon into six dessert dishes. Chill at least 2 hours. Garnish as desired.

Frozen Desserts

Chocolate Custard Ice Cream

Makes approximately 3 quarts.

 ⅔ cup Hershey's Cocoa
 2 cups granulated sugar
 2 tablespoons cornstarch
 ¼ teaspoon salt
 2 cups milk
 3 eggs
 1 tablespoon vanilla
 3 cups light cream
 2 cups heavy cream

Combine cocoa, 1½ cups of the sugar, cornstarch, and salt in a saucepan. Gradually stir in milk. Cook and stir over medium heat until mixture comes to a boil; boil and stir 1 minute. Remove from heat. Quickly beat eggs with remaining ½ cup sugar. Blend a small amount of the hot mixture into the beaten eggs; add to mixture in saucepan. Blend in vanilla and both creams. Chill. Freeze in ice cream freezer according to manufacturer's directions.

Chocolate-Strawberry Bombe

Makes 10 to 12 servings.

 ½ cup milk
 1½ teaspoons unflavored gelatin
 1 cup Hershey's Chocolate Flavored Syrup
 3 egg yolks, well beaten
 2 tablespoons butter or margarine
 1 teaspoon vanilla
   Strawberry Filling
 3 egg whites
 ⅓ cup granulated sugar
 1 cup heavy cream
 2 tablespoons confectioners' sugar
   Chocolate curls, optional
   Sliced strawberries, optional

Combine milk and gelatin in a medium saucepan. Let stand 3 to 4 minutes to soften gelatin. Add chocolate syrup and egg yolks. Cook over medium heat, stirring constantly, until mixture just begins to boil. Remove from heat. Stir in butter or margarine and vanilla. Pour into large bowl. Place plastic wrap directly onto surface of chocolate mixture. Chill until set.

Prepare Strawberry Filling.

Beat egg whites until foamy. Gradually add sugar and beat until stiff peaks form. Beat chocolate mixture on medium speed until smooth, about 30 seconds. Reduce speed to low. Blend in meringue.

Line a 1½-quart bowl with aluminum foil. Pour 1¼ cups of the chocolate mixture into the bowl. Carefully spoon Strawberry Filling over chocolate. Spoon in remaining chocolate. Cover. Freeze overnight.

Just before serving whip heavy cream with confectioners' sugar until stiff. Unmold frozen bombe onto a serving plate. Spread whipped cream over entire surface. Garnish with chocolate curls and sliced strawberries, if desired.

Strawberry Filling

 1 cup frozen nondairy whipped topping, thawed
   or 1 cup sweetened whipped cream
 ⅔ cup puréed, sweetened strawberries
 2 tablespoons light corn syrup

Combine whipped topping or whipped cream, sweetened strawberries, and corn syrup in a small bowl. Chill.

Frozen Chocolate-Almond Mousse

Makes 10 to 12 ½-cup servings.

 1⅓ cups (14-ounce can) sweetened condensed milk
 3 eggs, separated
 ½ cup (5.5-ounce can) Hershey's Chocolate Flavored Syrup
 ¼ teaspoon almond extract
 1 cup heavy cream*
   Additional whipped cream, chocolate curls, or sliced almonds, optional

Combine sweetened condensed milk and egg yolks in a small saucepan. Cook over low heat, stirring constantly, until mixture thickens slightly, about 10 minutes. Pour into large bowl; cover. Chill until mixture is completely cooled, about 30 minutes. Add chocolate syrup and almond extract; blend well.

Beat egg whites in small bowl until stiff but not dry. Fold egg whites into chocolate mixture. Whip cream until stiff. Fold whipped cream into chocolate mixture. Spoon mixture into parfait or dessert dishes. Freeze 2 hours or until firm. Top with desired garnish. Return leftovers to freezer.

*Do not substitute nondairy whipped topping.

Chocolate-Strawberry Bombe, above

Frozen Desserts

Chocoberry Loaf

Makes 10 to 12 servings.

  Cookie Crumb Crust
  3 3-ounce packages cream cheese, softened
  1 cup Hershey's Chocolate Flavored Syrup
  4½ cups frozen nondairy whipped topping, thawed
  ¾ cup sliced strawberries, puréed
  2 tablespoons light corn syrup

Prepare Cookie Crumb Crust. Set aside.

Whip 2 of the packages of cream cheese in small bowl. Gradually blend in chocolate syrup; beat until smooth. Fold in 3 cups of the whipped topping. Spoon half of the chocolate mixture into the prepared crust. Sprinkle with ½ cup crumbs reserved from crust. Freeze about 15 minutes. Chill remaining chocolate mixture.

Whip remaining package of cream cheese in small bowl. Blend in puréed strawberries and corn syrup until smooth. Fold in remaining 1½ cups whipped topping. Spoon strawberry mixture onto chocolate layer in loaf pan. Sprinkle with ½ cup crumb mixture; freeze about 15 minutes. Spoon remaining chocolate filling onto strawberry layer. Top with remaining crumbs; pat down lightly. Cover. Freeze several hours or overnight. Unmold about 10 minutes before serving. Peel off foil before slicing.

Cookie Crumb Crust

  3 cups chocolate creme-filled sandwich cookie crumbs
  ⅓ cup butter or margarine, melted

Combine ingredients in a small bowl. Pat ½ cup crumb mixture onto the bottom of a foil-lined 9 x 5 x 3-inch loaf pan. Freeze. Reserve remaining crumbs for between layers and top.

Cocoa-Rum Old Fashioneds

Makes 6 to 8 servings.

  ½ cup Hershey's Cocoa
  ½ cup granulated sugar
  1 teaspoon cinnamon
  2 cups heavy cream
  ½ to 1 teaspoon rum or rum extract
  1 cup crushed cinnamon sugar cookies (about 12 cookies)
  ½ cup flaked coconut
    Additional flaked coconut
    Red food color

Combine cocoa, sugar, and cinnamon in large bowl. Add heavy cream and rum or rum extract; beat until stiff. Fold in cookie crumbs and coconut. Spoon into old-fashioned glasses. Cover and freeze until firm. Before serving, mix coconut with a few drops red food color; stir to completely coat coconut. Sprinkle on top of each serving.

Individual Brownie Baked Alaskas

Makes 2 servings.

  ½ cup shortening
  1 cup granulated sugar
  1 teaspoon vanilla
  1 egg
  1 egg yolk
  2 tablespoons milk
  1 cup unsifted all-purpose flour
  ⅓ cup Hershey's Cocoa
  ½ teaspoon baking powder
  ¼ teaspoon salt
  ½ cup chopped almonds
  2 scoops mint-chocolate chip ice cream
    Meringue
    Chopped or sliced almonds

Cream shortening, sugar, and vanilla in a small bowl until light and fluffy. Add egg, egg yolk, and milk; blend well. In a separate bowl combine flour, cocoa, baking powder, salt, and almonds. Add flour mixture to creamed mixture; blend well. Spread batter evenly into a greased, 9-inch square baking pan. Bake at 350° for 25 to 30 minutes or until brownie begins to pull away from edges of pan. Cool in pan. Cut into 9 squares.

To assemble, place two brownie squares on an ungreased cookie sheet. Prepare Meringue. Place one scoop of ice cream on the center of each brownie. Cover ice cream and brownie completely with meringue. Garnish with chopped or sliced almonds. Bake at 450° for 4 to 5 minutes or until meringue is lightly browned. Serve immediately. (To make additional servings, prepare additional meringue, assemble, and bake as directed.)

Meringue

  1 egg white
  ⅛ teaspoon cream of tartar
  2 tablespoons granulated sugar

Beat the egg white and cream of tartar in small bowl until foamy. Gradually add sugar; continue beating at high speed until stiff peaks form.

Chocolate Syrup Homemade Ice Cream

Makes approximately 2½ quarts.

    2 envelopes unflavored gelatin
1½ cups milk
¾ cup granulated sugar
1½ cups (1-pound can) Hershey's Chocolate Flavored
    Syrup
    2 cups light cream
    2 tablespoons vanilla
    2 cups heavy cream

Sprinkle gelatin onto milk in a saucepan; let stand to soften gelatin, about 5 minutes. Add sugar; stir to blend. Cook, stirring constantly, until gelatin is dissolved. Remove from heat. Blend in chocolate syrup, light cream, and vanilla. Freeze according to one of the following methods:

Refrigerator-Freezer Method

Pour into a 9-inch square baking pan. Place in freezer until partially frozen. Whip heavy cream until stiff. Spoon chocolate mixture into chilled, large bowl; beat until smooth. Fold in whipped cream. Cover. Place bowl in freezer or pour into a 13 x 9 x 2-inch baking pan. Freeze several hours or until firm. Stir occasionally during the first hour. Garnish with sliced almonds and sweetened strawberries, if desired.

Electric or Crank-Type Freezer Method

Stir in heavy cream (unwhipped). Fill ice cream container two-thirds; position dasher. Cover can; place in freezer tub. Freeze according to manufacturer's directions.

Chocolate-Butter Pecan Ice Cream

Makes approximately 1½ quarts.

½ cup coarsely chopped pecans
    1 tablespoon butter
⅔ cup water
½ cup Hershey's Cocoa
1⅓ cups (14-ounce can) sweetened condensed milk
    2 teaspoons vanilla
    2 cups heavy cream

Sauté pecans in butter in a small saucepan over medium heat, stirring occasionally, for 2 to 3 minutes. Cool. Bring water to a boil in a small saucepan. Remove from heat and immediately add cocoa; blend well. Stir in sweetened condensed milk and vanilla. Pour into an 8-inch square baking pan. Freeze, stirring occasionally, until mushy.

Whip heavy cream in large bowl until stiff. Whip chocolate mixture in small, chilled bowl. Fold chocolate mixture into whipped cream. Blend in pecans. Pour into pan. Return to freezer. Freeze until firm. Stir occasionally during the first hour.

Peanut Butter Marble Cheese Dessert

Makes 10 to 12 servings.

    Chocolate Crumb Crust
    2 cups (12-ounce package) Reese's Peanut Butter
    Chips
½ cup milk
1⅓ cups (14-ounce can) sweetened condensed milk
    3 teaspoons vanilla
    4 3-ounce packages cream cheese, softened
    2 tablespoons lemon juice
    1 cup heavy cream

Prepare Chocolate Crumb Crust; freeze.

Combine peanut butter chips, milk, and ⅓ cup of the sweetened condensed milk in the top of a double boiler. Cook over low heat, stirring constantly, until chips are melted and mixture is thick and smooth. Remove from heat. Stir in 1 teaspoon of the vanilla. Cool to room temperature.

Beat cream cheese in large bowl until light and fluffy. Gradually beat in remaining 1 cup sweetened condensed milk, lemon juice, and 2 teaspoons vanilla.

Whip cream until stiff. Fold whipped cream into cooled peanut butter mixture. Reserve ½ cup peanut butter mixture.

Alternately pour remaining peanut butter and vanilla mixtures into crust, ending with vanilla. Spoon dollops of reserved peanut butter mixture on top. Swirl for a marbled effect. Freeze until firm. Remove from freezer 10 minutes before serving.

Chocolate Crumb Crust

1¼ cups graham cracker crumbs
¼ cup Hershey's Cocoa
¼ cup granulated sugar
¼ cup butter or margarine, melted

Combine all ingredients in a small bowl; blend thoroughly. Press mixture evenly on bottom and ½-inch up sides of a 9-inch springform pan. Freeze.

Microwave

Microwave Hints

Most microwave ovens today range between 600 and 700 watts, so the high setting is fairly standard. Lower levels of power are not standard; they will vary with various brands and models of microwave ovens. When lower powers are used in these recipes, they are listed according to percentage of power:

High	full power	600-700 watts
Medium-high	⅔ power	425-475 watts
Medium	½ power	300-350 watts
Low	⅓ power	175-225 watts
Warm		75-125 watts

Keep in mind that the cooking times given in the recipes are only guidelines; they will vary according to cooking pattern and wattage of your particular microwave oven. For this reason, rely on the desired result (i.e. microwave for 5 minutes, *or* until mixture boils) to determine "doneness."

Results are more consistent if food is stirred or rotated several times during microwave cooking. The cooking time for cookies, muffins, etc. is geared to the number of items called for in the recipe. If you are cooking fewer items, decrease the time; for more items, increase the time. All recipes have been tested in a 650 watt microwave oven.

Light Chocolate Pound Cake

Makes 12 to 14 servings.

　1 cup butter*
　3 cups granulated sugar
　½ cup shortening
　1 teaspoon vanilla
　5 eggs
　3 cups unsifted all-purpose flour
　6 tablespoons Hershey's Cocoa
　½ teaspoon baking powder
　½ teaspoon salt
　1 cup milk

Cream butter, sugar, shortening, and vanilla in large bowl until light and fluffy. Add eggs; beat well. In a separate bowl combine flour, cocoa, baking powder, and salt. Alternately add flour mixture and milk to creamed mixture. Beat until

thoroughly blended. Pour into a well-greased microwave Bundt pan. Place on a microwave rack or on an inverted saucer. Microwave on high (full power) for 20 to 22 minutes or until cake tester inserted comes out clean. (Turn one quarter turn every 6 minutes during cooking time.) Let stand 15 minutes covered with aluminum foil. Remove from pan and cool completely. Sprinkle with confectioners' sugar or glaze as desired.

*Do not substitute margarine in this recipe.

Microwave Chocolate Pudding

Makes 4 servings.

　⅔ cup granulated sugar
　¼ cup Hershey's Cocoa
　3 tablespoons cornstarch
　¼ teaspoon salt
2¼ cups milk
　2 tablespoons butter *or* margarine
　1 teaspoon vanilla

Combine sugar, cocoa, cornstarch, and salt in a medium-size glass bowl. Gradually stir in milk. Microwave on high (full power) for 5 minutes, stirring once half-way through cooking time. Microwave on high (full power) until mixture is cooked and thickened, about 1 to 2 minutes more. Stir in butter *or* margarine and vanilla. Pour into individual serving dishes. Press plastic wrap directly onto surface of pudding. Chill.

Cocoa Fudge Frosting

Makes approximately 2 cups.

　½ cup butter *or* margarine
　½ cup Hershey's Cocoa
3⅔ cups (1-pound box) confectioners' sugar
　⅓ cup milk
　1 teaspoon vanilla

Microwave butter *or* margarine in glass bowl on high (full power) until melted, about 1 minute. Stir in cocoa until smooth. Microwave on high (full power) until mixture boils, ½ to 1 minute. Add confectioners' sugar and milk. Beat with mixer until spreading consistency. Blend in vanilla. Spread while warm.

Microwave

Cocoa Upside-Down Cake

Makes 6 to 8 servings.

- 3 tablespoons butter *or* margarine
- ⅓ cup packed brown sugar
- 1 16-ounce can pineapple rings, drained
- ⅓ cup maraschino cherries, drained
- ¼ cup pecan pieces
- 1 cup unsifted all-purpose flour
- 1 cup granulated sugar
- ⅓ cup Hershey's Cocoa
- ¾ teaspoon baking soda
- ¼ teaspoon salt
- ¼ cup butter *or* margarine, softened
- ¾ cup sour cream
- 2 eggs
- 1 teaspoon vanilla

In a 2-quart microwave tube pan or 8-inch square glass dish, microwave the 3 tablespoons butter *or* margarine on high (full power) until melted, about ½ to 1 minute. Stir in brown sugar; spread evenly over bottom of pan. Arrange pineapple rings, cherries, and pecan pieces in a decorative design over mixture in pan; set aside.

Combine flour, sugar, cocoa, baking soda, and salt in a large bowl. Blend in ¼ cup butter *or* margarine, sour cream, eggs, and vanilla; beat 2 minutes on medium speed. Carefully pour over fruit and nuts in pan. Microwave on high (full power) for 8 to 10 minutes, turning pan one quarter turn every 3 minutes of cooking time, until top no longer appears moist. Let stand 15 minutes; cake should pull away from side of pan and cake tester inserted should come out clean. Immediately invert onto serving plate.

Cocoa Muffins

Makes 14.

- 1 cup unsifted all-purpose flour
- ⅔ cup granulated sugar
- ¼ cup Hershey's Cocoa
- 2 teaspoons baking powder
- ½ teaspoon salt
- ½ cup milk
- ¼ cup vegetable oil
- 1 egg, lightly beaten
- 1 cup raisins
- ½ cup chopped nuts

Combine dry ingredients in a glass bowl. Add milk, oil, and egg all at once; stir just until moistened. Fold in raisins and nuts. Fill 7 2½-inch paper muffin cups one-half full with batter; place in microwave cupcake or muffin maker. Microwave on high (full power) for about 2 to 2½ minutes, turning one quarter turn after 1 minute, 1½ minutes, and 2 minutes. Repeat with remaining batter. Serve warm.

Note: Cooking time for this recipe is geared to seven muffins. If making less at one time, cooking time should be shortened.

Autumn Mini Chip Ring

Makes 10 to 12 servings.

- ¾ cup unsifted whole wheat flour*
- ¾ cup unsifted all-purpose flour
- ¾ cup granulated sugar
- ½ cup packed brown sugar
- 1¼ teaspoons baking soda
- 2 teaspoons cinnamon
- ½ teaspoon salt
- 3 eggs
- ¾ cup vegetable oil
- 1½ teaspoons vanilla
- 2 cups grated carrot, apple, *or* zucchini, drained
- ¾ cup Hershey's Semi-Sweet Chocolate Mini Chips
- ½ cup chopped walnuts
  Cream Cheese Glaze

Combine flours, sugar, brown sugar, baking soda, cinnamon, and salt in a large bowl. In a separate bowl beat eggs, oil, and vanilla. Add to dry ingredients and blend. Stir in carrot, apple, *or* zucchini, Mini Chips, and walnuts. Pour into a well-greased 6-cup micro-proof ring or Bundt pan. Microwave immediately on microwave rack or inverted saucer on high (full power) for 13 to 15 minutes; turn dish one quarter turn every 3 minutes, or until cake tester inserted comes out clean. Cool for 30 minutes; remove from pan. Cool completely; spread with Cream Cheese Glaze.

*All-purpose flour may be substituted for whole wheat flour.

Cream Cheese Glaze

- 1 3-ounce package cream cheese, softened
- 1½ cups confectioners' sugar
- 1 tablespoon milk
- 1 teaspoon vanilla

Cream softened cream cheese until smooth in a small bowl. Blend in confectioners' sugar, milk, and vanilla. Beat until glaze is smooth and of spreading consistency.

Fresh Peach Coffee Cake

Makes 8 to 10 servings.

- ⅓ cup apricot *or* peach preserves
- 2 cups sliced fresh peaches*
- 1 tablespoon lemon juice
  Maraschino *or* dark, sweet cherries
- 1½ cups unsifted all-purpose flour
- ½ cup granulated sugar
- 1½ teaspoons baking powder
- ½ teaspoon salt
- ½ teaspoon ground cinnamon
- ½ cup butter *or* margarine
- 1 egg, lightly beaten
- ½ cup milk
- ½ teaspoon vanilla
- ½ cup Hershey's Semi-Sweet Chocolate Mini Chips

Line an 8 x 2-inch round glass baking dish with waxed paper. Spread apricot *or* peach preserves evenly in bottom. Toss peach slices with lemon juice; arrange with cherries in a decorative design in baking dish.

Combine flour, sugar, baking powder, salt, and cinnamon in a large bowl. Cut in butter *or* margarine until mixture resembles fine crumbs. In a separate bowl combine egg, milk, and vanilla; add to dry ingredients, stirring just until blended (batter will appear slightly lumpy). Add Mini Chips. Spread batter carefully over fruit. On a rack or inverted saucer microwave on high (full power) for 9 to 11 minutes, turning one quarter turn every 3 minutes of cooking time.

Microwave until top appears dry or cake tester inserted comes out clean. Let stand 10 minutes. Loosen cake from sides of pan; invert onto a serving plate; remove waxed paper. Serve warm.

*2 cups (1-pound can) peach slices, well drained, can be substituted.

Chocolate Cheese Pie

Makes 10 to 12 servings.

- Graham Cracker Crust
- 1 8-ounce package cream cheese
- ⅓ cup granulated sugar
- 2 tablespoons Hershey's Cocoa
- 1 egg
- 1 teaspoon vanilla
- 1 cup sour cream
- ¼ cup granulated sugar
- ½ teaspoon vanilla

Prepare Graham Cracker Crust; cool.

Microwave cream cheese in glass bowl until soft-ened, about ½ to 1 minute on medium (half power). Add ⅓ cup sugar and cocoa; blend well. Add egg and vanilla; beat well. Pour into crumb crust. Microwave on medium-high (two-thirds power) for 1½ minutes; turn dish one quarter turn. Cook for additional 1½ to 2½ minutes, or until set except for 1½-inch spot in center. Combine sour cream, ¼ cup sugar, and vanilla; spread evenly over cream cheese layer. Microwave on low (one-third power) just until topping is warm. Let stand covered with foil for 10 minutes; refrigerate until well chilled.

Graham Cracker Crust

- ¼ cup butter *or* margarine
- 1¼ cups graham cracker crumbs
- 2 tablespoons granulated sugar

Microwave butter *or* margarine on high (full power) until melted, about 30 seconds to 1 minute. Stir in graham cracker crumbs and sugar; press mixture on bottom and up sides of a 9-inch glass pie plate. Microwave on high (full power) 30 seconds; turn plate one quarter turn. Microwave until lightly browned, about 30 seconds.

Cocoa Brownies

Makes 10 to 12.

- 2 tablespoons shortening
- ⅓ cup butter *or* margarine
- ¼ cup plus 2 tablespoons Hershey's Cocoa
- 1 cup granulated sugar
- 2 eggs
- 1 cup unsifted all-purpose flour
- ¼ teaspoon baking powder
- ¼ teaspoon salt
- ½ teaspoon vanilla
- ½ cup chopped nuts

Melt shortening and butter *or* margarine in a medium glass bowl on high (full power), about 1 minute. Stir in cocoa until smooth; blend in sugar. Add eggs; beat well. Stir in remaining ingredients. Spread batter into lightly greased 8-inch round baking dish. Microwave on medium (half power) for 7 minutes, turning one quarter turn every 3 minutes. Microwave on high (full power) until puffed and dry on top, about 3 to 4 minutes. Cool until set. Cut into wedges. Serve brownie wedges topped with a scoop of ice cream and chocolate syrup, if desired.

Hershey Bar Swirl Cake

Makes 12 to 14 servings.

    1 cup butter *or* margarine
    2 cups granulated sugar
    1 teaspoon vanilla
    5 eggs
 2½ cups unsifted all-purpose flour
    ¾ teaspoon baking soda
    ¼ teaspoon salt
 1½ cups sour cream
    ¼ cup honey *or* light corn syrup
    ¾ cup chopped pecans
    1 (½ pound) Hershey's Milk Chocolate Bar,
       broken into pieces
    ½ cup (5½-ounce can) Hershey's Chocolate
       Flavored Syrup

Cream butter *or* margarine, sugar, and vanilla in large bowl. Add eggs; beat well. In a separate bowl combine flour, baking soda, and salt. Alternately add flour mixture and sour cream to creamed mixture. Stir honey *or* corn syrup and pecans into 2 cups of the batter. Set aside.

Microwave chocolate bar pieces and chocolate syrup in a glass bowl on high (full power) just until chocolate is melted, about 1 to 2 minutes. Blend chocolate into remaining batter. Pour into a greased 12-cup microwave Bundt pan. Spoon reserved mixture evenly over chocolate batter in pan. Place the pan on a microwave rack or an inverted saucer. Microwave 22 to 25 minutes on high (full power), turning one quarter turn every 5 minutes of cooking time, until cake tester inserted comes out clean. Cool 30 minutes. Remove from pan and cool completely. Glaze or frost as desired.

Hershey Bar Pie

Makes 8 servings.

       Chocolate Cookie Crust, cooled
    1 (½ pound) Hershey's Milk Chocolate Bar
    ⅓ cup milk
 1½ cups miniature marshmallows
    1 cup heavy cream

Prepare piecrust; set aside.

Break chocolate bar into pieces; place in a glass bowl. Add milk and miniature marshmallows. Microwave on high (full power) until chocolate and marshmallows are melted and mixture is thick and smooth, about 3 to 4 minutes; cool. Whip cream until stiff; fold into chocolate mixture. Spoon into crust. Cover and chill.

Chocolate Cookie Crust

    ½ cup butter *or* margarine
    1 cup granulated sugar
    1 egg
    1 teaspoon vanilla
 1¼ cups unsifted all-purpose flour
    ½ cup Hershey's Cocoa
    ¾ teaspoon baking soda
    ¼ teaspoon salt

Cream butter *or* margarine and sugar in large bowl until light and fluffy. Add egg and vanilla; beat well. In a separate bowl combine flour, cocoa, baking soda, and salt; add to creamed mixture. Shape into two 1½-inch thick rolls. Wrap in waxed paper and plastic wrap; chill several hours or overnight. Cut 1 roll into ⅛-inch slices; arrange with edges barely touching on bottom and up sides of a greased 9-inch glass pie plate. Microwave on medium (½ power) for 5 to 6 minutes (turning pie plate ¼ turn every 2 minutes of cooking time).

Chocolate Cookies

Leftover dough from above crust may be frozen or sliced for cookies. Slice roll ¼ inch thick. Place 10 cookies on waxed paper in circular formation. Microwave on medium (½ power) until just set, 4 to 5 minutes (turning pie plate ¼ turn every 2 minutes). Cookies will continue to cook after removal from microwave. Cool.

Favorite Hot Cocoa

Makes 4 servings.

    3 tablespoons Hershey's Cocoa
    5 tablespoons granulated sugar
       Dash salt
    3 tablespoons hot water
    2 cups milk
    ¼ teaspoon vanilla

Combine cocoa, sugar, salt, and hot water in a heat-proof glass pitcher (3 to 4 cup capacity). Microwave on high (full power) until boiling, about 1 to 1½ minutes. Add milk; cook on high (full power) until hot, about 1½ to 2 minutes. Stir in vanilla.

Single serving: Place 1 heaping teaspoon Hershey's Cocoa, 2 heaping teaspoons granulated sugar, and a dash of salt in a micro-proof coffee cup. Add 2 teaspoons cold milk; stir until smooth. Fill cup with milk; microwave on high (full power) until hot, about 1 to 1½ minutes. Stir to blend; serve.

Hershey Bar Swirl Cake, above

Microwave

Easiest-Ever Cocoa Fudge

Makes 64 1-inch squares.

3⅔ cups (1 pound) confectioners' sugar, sifted
½ cup Hershey's Cocoa
¼ cup milk
½ cup butter *or* margarine
1 tablespoon vanilla
½ cup chopped nuts, optional

Microwave confectioners' sugar, cocoa, milk, and butter *or* margarine on high (full power) until butter is melted, about 2 to 3 minutes; stir until smooth. Blend in vanilla and nuts. Spread into a buttered 8-inch square pan; cool. Cut into squares.

Rocky Road

Makes 64 1-inch squares.

2 cups (12-ounce package) Hershey's Semi-Sweet Chocolate Chips or Mini Chips
¼ cup butter *or* margarine
2 tablespoons shortening
5 cups (10½-ounce bag) miniature marshmallows
1 cup chopped nuts

Microwave chocolate chips, butter *or* margarine, and shortening on medium (½ power) until melted, about 5 to 7 minutes; stir until smooth. Add marshmallows and nuts; blend well. Spread evenly in a greased 8-inch square pan. Refrigerate until firm; cut into squares.

Frozen Peanut Butter Chip Dessert

Makes 9 servings.

Chocolate Cereal Crust
2 cups (12-ounce package) Reese's Peanut Butter Chips
½ cup milk
2 3-ounce packages cream cheese, softened
⅔ cup confectioners' sugar
3½ cups (8-ounce container) frozen nondairy whipped topping, thawed

Prepare crust; freeze.

Microwave peanut butter chips and milk in a 4-cup glass measuring cup or bowl on medium (half power) for 1½ minutes; stir and continue cooking until chips are melted (about 1 minute longer); cool about 5 minutes. Soften cream cheese on low (one-third power) for 3 to 4 minutes; beat with confectioners' sugar in a large bowl until smooth. Stir in peanut butter chip mixture; blend well. Fold in whipped topping. Pour into prepared pan; sprinkle with reserved cereal crust mixture. Freeze several hours or overnight. Cut into squares.

Chocolate Cereal Crust

¾ cup miniature marshmallows
½ cup Hershey's Chocolate Flavored Syrup
1 tablespoon butter
3 cups crisp rice cereal

Combine marshmallows, chocolate syrup, and butter in a glass measuring cup or bowl on high (full power) for 1 minute. Stir until marshmallows are melted; pour over cereal and stir until completely blended. Reserve ½ cup cereal mixture for top; press remaining cereal mixture into buttered or foil-lined 8 or 9-inch square pan. Freeze.

Black Magic Cake

Makes 10 to 12 servings.

1¾ cups unsifted all-purpose flour
2 cups granulated sugar
¾ cup Hershey's Cocoa
2 teaspoons baking soda
1 teaspoon baking powder
1 teaspoon salt
2 eggs
¾ cup strong black coffee *or* 1½ teaspoons instant coffee granules plus ¾ cup boiling water
¾ cup buttermilk *or* sour milk*
½ cup vegetable oil
1 teaspoon vanilla

Combine flour, sugar, cocoa, baking soda, baking powder, and salt in a large bowl. Add eggs, coffee, buttermilk *or* sour milk, oil, and vanilla; mix well. Fill two waxed paper-lined 8-inch round glass baking pans and about 8 paper-lined microwave muffin cups half full of batter. Microwave one cake layer at a time on medium (half power) for 7 minutes; then on high (full power) for 3 to 4 minutes or until a cake tester inserted comes out clean. (Turn one quarter turn every 3 minutes of cooking time.) Microwave cupcakes on medium (half power) for 3 to 4 minutes or until cake tester inserted comes out clean. (Turn one quarter turn every 1 minute of cooking time.) Cool completely. Remove from pans. Frost as desired.

To Sour Milk: Combine 2¼ teaspoons vinegar with milk to equal ¾ cup.

Beverages

Hot Cocoa for a Crowd

Makes approximately 4 quarts *or* 21 6-ounce servings.

- 1 cup Hershey's Cocoa
- 1½ cups granulated sugar
- ½ teaspoon salt, optional
- ¾ cup hot water
- 4 quarts milk
- 1 tablespoon vanilla

Blend cocoa, sugar, and salt in a 6-quart saucepan; gradually add hot water. Cook over medium heat, stirring constantly, until mixture begins to boil; continue cooking and stirring for 2 minutes. Add milk; heat thoroughly. Stir occasionally; do *not* boil. Remove from heat; add vanilla. Serve hot.

Cocoa Banana Special

Makes 2 servings.

- 1 small banana
- 3 tablespoons Hershey's Cocoa
- 3 tablespoons granulated sugar
- 1¾ cups milk

Slice banana into blender container; add cocoa and sugar, blending until smooth. Add ½ cup milk; blend until foamy. Add remaining milk; blend well. Serve immediately or store in refrigerator and stir before serving.

Variation

Add ¼ cup peanut butter to banana mixture; blend until smooth. Proceed as above.

Quickie Cocoa Drink

Makes 1 serving.

- 1 tablespoon granulated sugar
- 2 teaspoons Hershey's Cocoa
- 1 tablespoon very hot water
- 1 cup cold milk
- ¼ teaspoon vanilla, optional

Thoroughly blend sugar and cocoa in a cup. Add hot water; stir until sugar is dissolved and mixture is well blended. Add cold milk and vanilla; stir.

Chocolate Mint Refresher

Makes 1 serving.

- 4 or 5 peppermint candies
- 1 tablespoon Hershey's Cocoa
- 1 tablespoon granulated sugar
- 1 cup milk
- 1 scoop vanilla ice cream

Crush candies in blender. Add cocoa and sugar; blend well. Add milk and ice cream. Blend until smooth; serve immediately. Garnish with mint leaves, if desired.

Hurry-Up Hot Cocoa

Makes 1 serving.

- 1 tablespoon Hershey's Cocoa
- 1 to 2 tablespoons sugar, to desired sweetness
- Dash salt, optional
- Hot milk, approximately ¾ cup
- ⅛ teaspoon vanilla, optional

Combine cocoa, sugar, and salt in a cup; stir in hot milk to fill cup. Add vanilla, if desired; stir until blended.

Variations

Canadian Cocoa: Add ⅛ teaspoon maple extract.

Irish Mint Cocoa: Add ⅛ teaspoon pure mint *or* peppermint extract.

Orange Cocoa Cappucino: Add ⅛ teaspoon pure orange extract.

"Atole" (Peanut Butter Chip Drink)

Makes approximately 1½ quarts.

- 1 3⅛-ounce package vanilla pudding mix
- 2 cups milk
- 1 cinnamon stick
- 1 cup Reese's Peanut Butter Chips
- 4 cups milk

Blend pudding mix and 2 cups milk in a medium saucepan; add cinnamon stick. Cook, stirring constantly, until mixture thickens and comes to a boil. Remove from heat; blend in peanut butter chips, stirring until completely melted. Stir in remaining milk. To serve as cold drink, chill mixture thoroughly. To serve as hot drink, heat mixture; do *not* boil.

Spiced Hot Cocoa

Makes approximately 5 servings.

- ¼ cup Hershey's Cocoa
- ⅓ cup granulated sugar
- ½ teaspoon cinnamon
- ¼ teaspoon nutmeg
- ⅛ teaspoon salt
- ½ cup hot water
- 3½ cups milk
- 1 teaspoon vanilla
  - Dash cloves
  - Cinnamon sticks, optional

Combine cocoa, sugar, cinnamon, nutmeg, and salt in a saucepan; blend in hot water. Bring to boil over medium heat, stirring constantly; boil and stir 2 minutes. Add milk; heat to serving temperature, stirring occasionally. Do *not* boil. Remove from heat; add vanilla and cloves. Beat with a rotary beater until foamy. Serve hot. Garnish with a cinnamon stick, if desired.

Frosty Chocolate Shake

Makes approximately 5 cups.

- 1 cup water
- 1⅓ cups (14-ounce can) sweetened condensed milk
- ½ cup smooth peanut butter *or*
  - 2 medium ripe bananas
- ¼ cup Hershey's Cocoa
- 1 teaspoon vanilla
- 3 cups ice cubes

Combine all ingredients except ice in order listed in blender container; blend until smooth. Add ice cubes, 1 cup at a time, blending until smooth after each addition. Serve.

Perked Mocha Cocoa

Makes 4 8-ounce servings.

- 2½ cups cold water
- ¼ cup Hershey's Cocoa
- ⅓ cup granulated sugar
- 3 tablespoons ground coffee
- ⅛ teaspoon salt
- 1⅓ cups milk
- ½ teaspoon vanilla

Reserve 1 cup water; pour remaining water into percolator. Combine cocoa, sugar, coffee, and salt in a small bowl; pour into percolator basket. Assemble percolator; pour reserved water over cocoa mixture in basket. Stir until all water passes through; plug in percolator. Allow to perk completely and finish dripping. Meanwhile, heat milk in small saucepan over medium heat; stir in vanilla. Pour ⅓ cup warm milk into four serving mugs; fill with mocha cocoa.

Chocolate-Strawberry Cooler

Makes 2 servings.

- ¼ cup sweetened strawberries
- 1 tablespoon Hershey's Cocoa
- 1 tablespoon granulated sugar
- 1½ cups milk
- ½ cup chilled club soda
  - Whipped cream, optional
  - Fresh strawberries, optional

Combine sweetened strawberries, cocoa, and sugar in blender container; blend well. Add milk and club soda; blend. Garnish with a dollop of whipped cream and a fresh strawberry.

Hot Cocoa Mix

Makes 10 cups.

- 3 cups confectioners' sugar
- 3 cups nonfat dry milk crystals
- 2 cups miniature marshmallows
- 1 cup nondairy creamer
- 1 cup Hershey's Cocoa

Thoroughly combine ingredients in a bowl. Store in airtight container.

Single Serving: Place ¼ cup mixture in cup; add 6 ounces boiling water. Stir until well blended.

Chocolate Refresher

Makes 4 1-cup servings.

- ¼ cup granulated sugar
- ¼ cup Hershey's Cocoa
- ½ cup (3¾-ounce package) vanilla instant pudding and pie filling mix
- 2 cups milk
- 1 teaspoon vanilla
- 8 ice cubes

Combine sugar, cocoa, and pudding mix in blender container; blend well. Add ½ cup milk; blend thoroughly, scraping sides occasionally. Add remaining milk, vanilla, and ice cubes; blend at high speed until ice is crushed and mixture is thoroughly blended. Serve immediately or store in refrigerator.

Frosty Chocolate Shake, above
Chocolate-Strawberry Cooler, above
Spiced Hot Cocoa, above

Index